A Natural Year

A Natural Year

The Tranquil Rhythms and Restorative Powers of Irish Nature Through the Seasons

MICHAEL FEWER

MERRION
PRESS

First published in 2020 by
Merrion Press
10 George's Street
Newbridge
Co. Kildare
Ireland
www.merrionpress.ie

Illustrations and photographs by Michael Fewer

© Michael Fewer, 2020

9781785373183 (Paper)
9781785373190 (Kindle)
9781785373206 (Epub)
9781785373213 (PDF)

British Library Cataloguing in Publication Data
An entry can be found on request

Library of Congress Cataloging in Publication Data
An entry can be found on request

Cover design and typesetting by River Design

Front and back cover images: © Michael Fewer and Shutterstock

For my grandson, James Michael Fewer

Acknowledgements
This little book would not have come into being
without the support and inspiration of my wife,
Teresa, the advice of Jonathan Williams, and the
enthusiasm of Conor Graham and his colleagues at
Merrion Press.

CONTENTS

FOREWORD

It was in the late 1980s on the Aran Islands, when
taking trainee primary-school teachers – who were
there to brush up their Irish – on nature walks,
that it dawned on me that this particular sort of
thing was quite a useless exercise in many ways.
How could these students from the east of Ireland
feel any excitement at seeing the wonderful bloody
cranesbill, when they had no knowledge of its more
modest relation Herb Robert, a common plant
found in hedges and woodlands countrywide? Or
indeed expect them to be mightily impressed with
sightings of choughs with their brilliant red legs and
bills, when most of them didn't know the difference
between a rook and a jackdaw?

So, when I got the opportunity to present a whole
series of wildlife episodes for the then enormously
popular children's programme *The Den* at the end of
the 1990s, I made sure that the common residents
of my back garden were the stars. These were five-
minute weekly slots on such interesting creatures
as bumblebees, bluebottles, snails, centipedes,
woodlice, etc., all of whom performed splendidly
once the cameras started rolling. Ladybirds obligingly
fell into my upturned umbrella when I shook the
leaves on the tree. Spiders – great big hunting ones
– were always in my pitfall traps on inspection in

the morning, or so it appeared to the viewer. And as the episodes of *Creature Feature* (all fifty of them) were shown on repeat for the following five years, a whole generation of younger children – not to mention university students lounging at home looking at afternoon telly in those halcyon pre-internet and laptop days – became aware of and interested in what could be found just outdoors wherever they were.

We only conserve the things we love, and we can only love the things we understand. *An rud is annamh is iontach*, perhaps, but not when it was once *fliúrseach*, as our corncrakes and breeding curlews were until relatively recently. The ability to notice things and the curiosity to ask questions are the marks of a scientist, no matter what age they are or live in. But being able to communicate so well that the viewer, listener or reader immediately wants to go and experience what is being described, this is a much rarer talent. Michael Fewer has always been curious, always been aware of his surroundings, as is attested to by his many publications over the years. In this book he allows the reader to share what has made the day special for him as he looks out the window or walks through the local fields. It is a real celebration of nature.

Éanna Ní Lamhna

INTRODUCTION

The recent publication of startling statistics about
the detrimental effect humankind is having on the
flora and fauna of our planet has been a serious
'wake-up' call to all. The danger to the earth posed by
human activities has been known for decades. In his
introduction to *Far from Paradise: The Story of Man's Impact
on the Environment*, published as long ago as 1986, John
Seymour wrote:

> the purpose of this book ... is to decide not
> what is ethical about mankind's treatment
> of other forms of life but whether, as
> an increasing number of our people are
> beginning to believe, mankind's present
> exploitation of his planet is unsustainable.
> Can we continue to live as we are living, and
> work as we are working, for more than a
> limited number of generations?

Scientific data assembled over recent decades provides
solid evidence that we cannot.

At one time all humanity lived in intimate contact
with the natural world, and aspects of nature were
central themes in art and literature: from the Old
Testament's Song of Solomon onwards through
Greek and Roman literature, nature is frequently
celebrated; Shakespeare was sufficiently in touch with

his natural surroundings that his writings mention more than fifty bird species by name. In Ireland we had no industrial revolution, and so the majority of our population remained in touch with 'the land' well into the twentieth century. A creeping but inexorable change, however, occurred over the last half-century in the relationship between ourselves, particularly the increasing number of us who live in cities, and the natural world, with which we used to live in close harmony. Our ability to remain in touch with and be a part of nature as it weaves its strong, magic, cyclical spells has radically declined. Spending much of our time in the comfortable, artificial micro-climates of houses, cars or workplaces, our experience of the outside world is less and less an essential part our lives.

If we as individuals wish to have any impact in redressing the damage our civilisation has done, we must begin by reconnecting with nature. Those who do reach out to the natural world will find that many new and long-forgotten gifts await them; as the naturalist John Burroughs put it, 'We always have nature with us, and it is an inexhaustible storehouse of wonderments that move the heart, appeal to the mind, and fire the imagination; active observance of it provides health and joy and stimulus to the intellect from childhood to old age.'

Two thousand years ago, the Roman writer and naturalist Pliny the Elder wrote of the destructive power of nature, but added, 'Earth, however, is kind, gentle, indulgent, always a servant to man's needs, productive when compelled to be, or lavish of her own accord. What scents and tastes, what juices, what things to touch, what colours!'

Nature's beauty, to be found in the skies, in the landscape, and in its rich and varied flora and fauna, is always changing, by the hour, from morning to evening, from season to season. You don't have to travel to Central America or Africa, helping to fill the stratosphere with pollutants, to experience it. The extraordinary and the exotic in nature can be found, for those who look carefully, even in our backyards. For those who cannot get away to the Galapagos, Antarctica or Borneo, there are many hidden riches of the natural world to be discovered in our immediate surroundings, but only if we consciously slow down and open our eyes.

Myself and my wife, Teresa, are fortunate enough to share an interest in the natural world, onto which we have two windows: our south Dublin suburban home, and our country cottage in County Waterford. Each of these places, through their gardens, nearby hillsides, parks and seashores, delight us, raise our spirits, soothe and heal, and provide a reassuring solidity to our lives. We are not naturalists. We just enjoy nature and are curious about it, and have come to realise that the more one looks, the more one sees. I wrote this book, woven around entries in my journal, to attempt to share some of the stress-relieving pleasure Teresa and I get from observations and explorations of our natural world over a twelve-month period.

Although we live in an ordinary semi-detached house in suburban Dublin, we have three good nature habitats nearby. We overlook, from our back windows, a half-acre field, beyond which, eighty metres away, is a small wood of mature beech trees; what we like to call 'the Spinney'. The trees in the

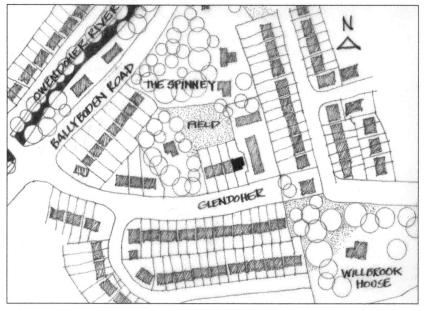

Glendoher today

Spinney were probably planted by Seán Keating, the painter (1889–1977), who built a house for himself and his family there in 1935, on the site of an old water mill. Eighty metres to the south-east of our house are the remains of Sir Frederick Moore's gardens at Willbrook House. Moore (1857–1949) was the curator of the Royal Botanic Gardens in Glasnevin for forty years, after which he spent a long retirement with his wife Phyllis in Willbrook House,

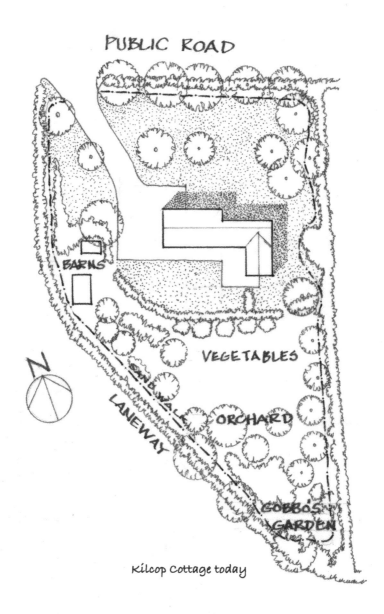

PUBLIC ROAD

BARNS

VEGETABLES

N

SIDE B WALL

LANEWAY

ORCHARD

GOBBO'S GARDEN

Kilcop Cottage today

lovingly tending their gardens, which were renowned for their trees, shrubs and plants. After he died, she continued with this work until her death in 1976. The property has been in private ownership since then, and what remains of the gardens are extant. To the west of our home, deep in a tree-shrouded ravine, is the Owendoher River, a mountain stream which flows off the northern slopes of Cruagh Mountain, providing a hidden, linear nature reserve. Our surroundings are not unique, however: there are few suburban areas that do not have similar 'green' areas nearby, such as urban parks, old gardens, leftover parcels of land, railway cuttings and old churchyards.

The nearby foothills of the Dublin Mountains provide a wilderness 'annex' to our home. Over the years Ticknock and Hellfire Hill, ten to fifteen minutes away by car, have become much-loved resorts for our outings to the semi-wild, and they have provided us with enormous pleasure over the years.

In the late 1970s Teresa and I bought an acre field in County Waterford, close to Waterford Harbour. We built a tiny cottage on it, and it became a great hideaway from Dublin urban life. Nearby, at Woodstown, there is a long cockleshell-strewn beach, a place that is deeply engrained in my family mythology, and which, somehow, has avoided the kind of developments that have spoiled other popular seaside places. Also close by is the fishing village of Dunmore East, where we could enjoy swimming, coastal exploration and mackerel fishing in summertime. At the time we built our cottage, there was only one house, a 200-year-old farmhouse, nearby. Since then, the surrounding area has seen the erection of nine homes, but there are still plenty of fields, fox coverts and woods close by.

Observations of 'ordinary' nature from our Dublin and Waterford homes, through a typical year, are offered here in the hope that they will inspire curiosity about that fascinating wild world that lives quietly in parallel with our twenty-first century digital, mechanised world, and provide a sure source of tranquillity to sooth our sometimes frenetic lifestyles.

January

*The country is more of a wilderness, more of a wild solitude,
in the winter than in the summer. The wild comes out. The
urban, the cultivated, is hidden …*

– John Burroughs

Waterhen

WINTER SEEMS TO GET LONGER AND DARKER the older one gets, and I celebrate and delight in any signs I come across of its approaching end and the longed-for beginning of spring. In the pre-dawn darkness it is a joy, hearing from the warmth of my bed, our early birds beginning to test their vocal cords, tentatively, as if self-consciously rehearsing for the full-scale dawn chorus they will take part in before many weeks have passed. The blackbird quietly tries out, without much success initially, a series of phrases. He keeps trying, however, with long pauses between each attempt, which leave me wondering if he has flown away. But then he starts up, attempting once again to get it right. Towards the end of January his song improves appreciably and the early morning rehearsals get less tentative. Outside my window, the blackbird is joined by the wren and the robin, whose enthusiasm needs no rehearsal. Pliny the Elder wrote that there is not a musical instrument devised by the cunning and art of man that can afford more music than the robin can produce.

Although each of our days, after 21 December, is a few minutes longer than the previous, the dark nights seem to drag on relentlessly and unchanged, for quite a while. January is a strange, slow sort of month, gripping autumn with one hand and spring with the other, standing motionless in frigid neutrality. The month is named after the Roman Janus, a human king who became a god, but deification caused him to develop two faces, one looking back to the old year, the other looking forward. The Anglo-Saxon name for January was *Wulfmonath*, the month when starving wolves were driven to descend, desperate and ferocious, on human settlements. Only plants like the crocus and the snowdrop brave January's temperatures, the crocus giving us colour that is astonishingly vivid against the surrounding greys, and the snowdrop, which gleams bright and new, offering hope that spring is near.

I have never forgotten the words Shakespeare used to describe the winter season in *As You Like It*:

> Blow, blow, thou winter wind!
> Thou are not so unkind
> As man's ingratitude.

And in *Love's Labour's Lost*:

> When icicles hang by the wall,
> And Dick, the shepherd, blows his nail,
> And Tom bears logs into the hall,
> And milk comes frozen home in pail …

When the days dawn bright and clear, however, January has many gifts to bring. It is a good month for tackling the hills for a walk, and if it has been frosty, usually boggy terrain is firm and lightly crunchy underfoot. We are fortunate to live near the Dublin Mountains, and we have a choice of hills on which to stretch our legs. Nearby, Ticknock is a particularly inspiring place after a light fall of snow. The outlook down to the dark, dirty-looking city makes one so grateful to be high up in a glistening landscape, and the myriad sparkles in the soft dry snow would brighten any spirits. Teresa likes it when the snow is fresh and a couple of inches thick; she says it's like walking on a duvet. A particular bonus of these conditions is the impossibility, if you watch out for them, of missing the prints left by passing fauna, prints that are not readily visible in normal conditions.

fox

red deer

While most bird species can be relatively easily spotted, even at a distance, because they can make an escape by taking to the air, many of our small corps of mammals, owing to aeons of human predation, tend to be secretive and nocturnal. Often their presence in a particular area can be discerned only by the tracks they leave, or indications of their feeding or grooming, or from as prosaic a matter as their droppings. Some animals, like humans, move from place to place in a fixed routine, and often this means that their frequently used routes can be identified. An extreme example of this is perhaps cattle moving every day from the field where they have been grazing to where they are milked; they walk in single file and wear down the grass to a narrow, bare earth path. It is rarely this extreme in the case of wild animals because they are much lighter on their feet, but it is often possible to see clearly the habitual route a badger takes through long grass, and the tunnel in vegetation the animal makes through a hedge or under a barbed wire fence.

Being able to identify what animal left what prints makes it easy to get an idea of the variety of species that frequent the countryside when you are not there. John Burroughs wrote, 'The snow is a great tell-tale, and blabs as effectively as it obliterates. I go into the woods, and know all that has happened. I cross the fields, and if only a mouse has visited his neighbour, the fact is chronicled.' The best time to read prints in the snow is when it is fresh and the cover is no thicker than an inch or so; in these conditions the prints are well defined without any distortion or blurring. It is also important to try to get out before other walkers and their dogs complicate the situation!

Even if the snowfall occurred only a few hours before, it can be surprising to see how much traffic there has been. Once you learn what the footprints of foxes, hares, rabbits and deer look like, the remaining question that one has to work out is the sequence of passage – which animal came first? On heathery Ticknock, well away from the telecommunications masts, there are often numerous tracks of birds in the snow, particularly those of the red grouse; by carefully observing what you find, you may be able to discern the shape of the smaller female's foot from the longer, larger male's.

Hellfire Hill is nearby and is another great place for us to take a walk. Recently, walking in a light covering of snow on the west side of the hill, where less people stray, I was surprised to see how many deer had been active there. The snow showers had been about dawn, three hours before I got there, but the forestry road was full of deer prints, and there were places where you could see that they had dug in the snow to get at grass. There were also lots of rabbit prints, and a fox had been about.

Foot or paw prints are only one of the signs of an animal's passing that you can detect if you are observant; the term 'spoor', an Afrikaans word, means the wide range of signs that wild animals leave behind, such as prints, droppings, signs of grazing, tufts of fur or bark nibbled off a young tree. Sometimes the spoor can tell a story. On one frosty morning in late January on Ticknock I came across the oval-shaped prints of what I took to be a fox. The fox is still a hunted animal, and I could see that, most of the time, it had placed its rear foot precisely in the footprint of its front foot, to reduce its spoor by 50 per cent. I followed it for about forty metres, and then it looked as if the animal had speeded up; the prints were blurred and it seemed as if the fox was kicking up flurries of snow in its wake. The confused trail ended in a hollow where there was much disturbed snow, a tuft of fur, and small patches of frozen blood. I was able to see that at this particular point the fox's trail had intersected with that of a rabbit, which had run fast for the last few moments only to be caught by the fox. Leading out of the hollow were only the fox's footprints, a little deeper than before, because he was carrying the rabbit, but reverting to halving his spoor again. I followed him, but the spoor disappeared into a maze of rocks and gorse. By learning more about these signs that animals have been about, we can enrich our outdoor explorations and get a glimpse into aspects of their way of life.

You don't have to wait for snow to give you a chance of seeing what has passed by before you; wet ground, muddy patches and, indeed, certain kinds of vegetation can all display signs of an animal's passing. To immerse oneself in the art of identifying spoor is to add an entirely new dimension to one's countryside wanderings. It is useful to arm yourself with an appropriate book, such as the *Hamlyn Guide to Animals Tracks, Trails and Signs*, or *The Nature Tracker's Handbook* by Nick Baker, because once you begin to look carefully at the ground, you will be surprised at how much you will find that cries out to be identified.

One bird that is always active in the early weeks of the year is the raven, because these birds appear to start their courtship in the winter months. Ravens contrive to have their young at the same time as lambing occurs on the hillsides, and so must start the process earlier than most birds. Lambing provides them with nutrient-rich placentas scattered about the fields, perfect food for their hungry young nestlings. Most farmers hate ravens. When a lamb is born with a serious defect, it is often abandoned by its mother, leaving it to the cruelty of nature. Ravens will concentrate on these, but if there are no sickly lambs about, they can often gang up on a healthy lamb and peck out its eyes or tongue; a blind or tongueless lamb will not survive for long, and as soon as it is dead, the birds will move in, and quickly and expertly disembowel the corpse. Ravens are protected birds, and before a farmer can think of shooting them, he or she has to apply for a permit.

Ravens are, however, only doing what nature dictates. I have great *grá* for these big birds, and have been fortunate on a number of memorable occasions to observe their spectacular aerial displays. On Hellfire Hill one January morning, I had been hearing the characteristic 'cronking' in the distance, a bit like a dog barking, all the way around the hill, and spotted one raven flying above the trees on the west side. A little later, however, I heard a series of calls that ranged from the familiar deep and visceral cronk to an almost melodious 'Cooook' and a harsh 'Kraaaak', and a trio of ravens flying in close formation came into view above me, jinking and changing places, obviously agitated. It looked like a love triangle, but soon one of them detached from the group, or was forcibly removed, I could not tell, leaving the remaining pair to embark on a series of circuits like ballroom dancers, formating closely together, so close at times that I wondered if, like swifts, they actually mate on the wing? They also performed that manoeuvre that I have only ever seen ravens do, flipping over onto their backs and then returning to normal flight, an aerobatic trick that allows them to see directly down. At one stage this pair seemed to briefly fly mirrored, one flying normally and the other flying upside down above it, calling sweetly to each other all the while. As they disappeared over the trees, I continued my walk with my spirits greatly raised.

ravens

Glendoher, 3 January
Getting out of the car in front of the house, I caught
sight of a bird flying quite high, but not too far
to clearly observe its shape, and that its belly was
a speckled light grey. As it went over the roof of
the house, it folded its wings against its flanks and
dropped like a stone, vertically, disappearing behind
the roof. At that moment I realised that it must be
a peregrine falcon – the swiftness of the dive, the
verticality of it, and reviewing the form of the bird
and the height it was flying at convinced me. I ran
into the house and up the stairs to the back room to
see if there was any activity in the field, but everything
was still, there was nothing to see or hear. A short
time before the trees would have been full of noisy
magpies and wood pigeons, and the usual robin,
hedge sparrow and tits would have been flitting about
the garden. Now there was no movement whatever,
no bird in sight. The peregrine is the fastest bird in
the world, and a species that almost became extinct
in Ireland a few decades ago. The bird dives at up
to 300km per hour to strike its prey, often a wood
pigeon, killing it instantly. This particular peregrine
was probably somewhere in the undergrowth of the
Spinney, already plucking its prey. It was a wonder to
see one of these dramatic raptors in the air over my
home.

Glendoher, 8 January
Two mornings ago I watched from the breakfast table
as a darting and jinking gang of a dozen magpies put
on a vigorous aerial display in the Spinney treetops.
Fluttering and swooping, circling and perching, they

magpie

moved as a team from branch to branch in an attempt
to dislodge a much larger bird that was perched
in the middle of the Spinney. Eventually the large
bird, which I guessed was the resident sparrowhawk,
launched into the air, and after making a few
threatening lunges at the magpies, it flew snootily and
slowly away.

This morning, however, I was present for a similar
but more extended show, and watched it from the
beginning through binoculars. As usual, when the
winter sun illuminates the branchy fringe at the top of
the Spinney and pushes the shadows downwards along
their trunks, a flock of wood pigeons arrives to warm
themselves on their everyday morning perches. Before
long, first a couple, and then more magpies arrive,
circling around the pigeons and making threatening
darts at them from branch to branch. Soon, as they do
every day, the wood pigeons gave up trying to get a bit
of warmth and depart for a more peaceful existence
somewhere else.

Having sent the docile wood pigeons packing,
instead of taking their place as usual, the magpies

worked their way westwards along the Spinney, some
hopping from branch to branch, others circling and
diving, and it was clear that another occupant of
the trees had become the subject of their attention.
Suddenly, a large, chunky white-breasted sparrowhawk
burst out of cover and made an aerial lunge at the
magpies. A brief aerial dogfight followed, with the
magpies getting more animated, ducking and dodging
their victim, and seeming to enjoy every minute of it.
The sparrowhawk was fast, but had no effect on the
magpies, and after a few passes it perched again, up on
the western end of the Spinney. It looked magnificent
through the binoculars, its strongly barred, light-
coloured breast, its long yellow legs and grey-capped
head highlighted in the low sun. The magpies
continued their harassment, and after a few minutes,
like the wood pigeons, the sparrowhawk just gave up
and took himself elsewhere, away from the racket.

But there was more to come. Having successfully
flushed the pigeons and the sparrowhawk, the pied
teddy boys started concentrating on the lower levels of
the Spinney, and it wasn't long before a male kestrel
was flushed out. It flew straight towards my window
and over the roof of the house. What a show! Twenty
minutes later, the magpie gang had gone elsewhere to
see what trouble they could stir up.

The raven was once persecuted almost out of
existence, mainly for the reasons mentioned above,
but also because it was thought to be an evil spirit.
In recent decades, however, there has been a great
increase in raven numbers, and many pairs have
moved into suburbia, where it is not unusual, if you
know what to look for, to see them. One or more
of them are frequently involved in skirmishes with

grey-backed crows and magpies over the Spinney. In the last two days, however, taking a walk up through a housing estate to our local park, I twice heard, and then spotted ravens. They seem to be preparing for nesting in two tall stands of pine trees, one of them in the old garden of Sir Frederick Moore, about a hundred metres from our front door.

Glendoher, 12 January

Buds are beginning to appear on some plants, and it is a delight when the snowdrops come out; no garden should be without them, if only as a gentle reassurance that spring is on the way. The magnolia is one of the early trees to produce fat buds; its waxy blossoms later on are a joy, if short-lived.

The final great indicator for Teresa and me happens when a morning dawns clear skied, with the early sun making a halo of gold of the myriad bare branches of the Spinney treetops. We glory in this heart-warming sight, and spend our time at the breakfast table pointing out to each other nuances of this new and restoring morning light.

It seems a chore to get oneself out for a walk on a dark January morning; I tend to stick to the nearby foothills for a stretching walk, or a circuit from my front door that takes in a local park. On one such walk I was passing through the park when I was sure I spotted a dipper, one of our most fascinating birds, diving into the gently cascading mountain stream that flows through the park. I kept my eye on the spot in the water where I thought he had disappeared, and stopped close to it, just two metres above the water. There I stood, watching and wondering, but no bird surfaced. I must have mistaken a late falling leaf for the dipper, and I was just about to continue my walk when, out of the corner of my eye, I caught a flash of brilliant white through the winter branches downstream. What I first thought was a swan flying just above the stream's surface was approaching upriver. At this time of year all the landscape is dun-coloured, and the brilliant white of the gently flexing long wings stood out dramatically, but it was not a swan, it was a little egret.

I stood stock still as the bird came closer and closer. It alighted in the stream just metres away, and crouching over, began to search for small fish or snails below some herbs overhanging the stream's edge. Its dagger-like black beak and black legs contrasted with its whiter-than-white plumage, and what I found remarkable was how the bird's legs were shivering as if it found the water cold. It did seem to succeed in getting a few morsels, but then it opened its wings, launched itself into the air and disappeared upriver.

The name egret is from the French *aigrette*, or small heron; this beautifully proportioned bird was once common in these islands, but, because of climate and predation by man, it began its descent into local extinction as early as the fifteenth century. It was regarded as a delicacy by the aristocracy, and was often included on royal menus: the feast to celebrate the enthronement of George Neville as Archbishop of York in 1465 included 1,000 little egrets among the 'poultry' served. The birds' long feathers were sought-after for plumes to decorate hats in the eighteenth century: in the first three months of 1885, 750,000 egret skins were sold in London alone. The bird was rare even in southern Europe by the 1950s, but new conservation laws saw numbers increase strongly, and by 1997 the bird turned up in coastal regions of Cork, Waterford and Wexford. In the last twenty years it has had an amazing recovery in Ireland, and can now be found in most coastal counties. I spotted my first 'park' egret in nearby Marlay Park in 2018, but, until this, I had never been so close to one.

It was a remarkable coincidence that the American landscape poet Mary Oliver had died, at the age of eighty-three, only a week before this encounter. I remembered some evocative lines that she had written in her poem 'Egrets' and looked them up again when I got home:

> And that's how I came
> to the edge of the pond:
> black and empty
> except for a spindle
> of bleached reeds
> at the far shore
> which, as I looked,
> wrinkled suddenly
> into three egrets …
> a shower
> of white fire!
> Even half-asleep they had
> such faith in the world
> that had made them …
> tilting through the water,
> unruffled, sure,
> by the laws
> of their faith not logic,
> they opened their wings
> softly and stepped
> over every dark thing.

Glendoher, 14 January

The goldfinches have finally returned to Glendoher. Last year when we put the nyjer seeds out, by some magical communication system known only to birds, goldfinches, which rarely grace our garden, turned up within a day, and feasted on the seeds for a week, three and four at a time perched on the feeder. This winter we hung the feeder out again in November, but except for one visit by one bird, we saw no goldfinches at all until last week. As if they have just arrived in the neighbourhood, three pairs have been constantly coming to the feeder, with three queuing in the Himalayan birch tree while the other three feed. It is such a joy to see such bright colours against the garden's drab background, but it is impossible to fully appreciate the wonderful plumage of the male goldfinch unless you see it up close, through binoculars.

With the goldfinch feeding on the nyjer seed this year is the tiny pink-capped redpoll; five of these little beauties, an unusual, odd number, have been coming for the last two days. The redpolls are particularly covetous birds, constantly fighting with one another in intricate and fast aerial combats for a place on the feeder; though there is enough space to take four of

these tiny ruffians, rarely will those feeding put up
with more than three. Birdwatch Ireland says that the
redpoll is 'a widespread breeding species, mainly in
upland areas', but although I spend a lot of time in
our nearby 'upland areas', I have never once seen a
redpoll there. Maybe it is because they usually breed
in coniferous plantations, and although one will
often hear the twittering of the birds that frequent
conifers, it is always difficult to see them. In winter,
and particularly when food becomes scarce in the
coniferous plantations, redpolls come down to the
lowlands seeking a variety of seeds, and nyjer seeds
seem to be a favourite.

Glendoher, 15 January
When the temperature drops and frost appears, the
number of bird species frequenting our garden seems
to increase. I was surprised one morning, with the
temperature below zero, to see tiny goldcrests and
siskins in the conifers behind the wall, and later
in the morning an amazing flock of about sixty to
seventy goldfinches flying over the field, east to west.
I hoped they would wheel and come back to our
feeder, but they continued to swoop along, their gay
colours brightly reflecting the sun, to the tall trees
at the west of the field. They stayed there for ten or
fifteen minutes, busily moving about and feeding
in the upper branches. Only when a visiting seagull
flew too close did they move on, flowing across to a
neighbouring tree. About two dozen came to the tall
conifer at the eastern end of the field and dropped
down to perch in the fronds; they were beautiful
to see, the low morning sun picking up their light-
coloured undersides as they hung upside down to get

at choice titbits. Then a magpie came chattering past
and set them off again, westward ho!

> Sometimes goldfinches one by one will drop
> From low hung branches; little space they stop;
> But sip, and twitter, and their feathers sleek;
> Then off at once, as in a wanton freak:
> Or, perhaps, to show their black, and golden
>   wings,
> Pausing upon their yellow flutterings.

– John Keats, 'I stood tip-toe upon a little hill'

January will often bring other interesting visitors to
our garden, including blackcap pairs, greenfinches
and redwings, those small thrushes that are visitors
from Iceland and Scandinavia, a mere 1,500
kilometres away to the north-west and north-east.
Looking out the back window for about five minutes
at dusk one frosty evening, I was lucky enough to see
a large flock of redwings heading from the Spinney in
the direction of St Enda's Park, where they will roost
in the middle of one of the extensive lawns. I did a
rapid count which came to more than 250 birds.

A pair of bullfinches turn up every year and
spend some time stripping the new growth from the
cherry tree. These birds have plumage that belongs
to the tropics, but because of their shyness, they are
not easily seen close up. The male is dolled up in a
shocking red/pink and wears a jet-black cap, while the
female is a more refined sandy brown. Just one pair
seems to visit us, and we always see them together.

The winter in these parts often brings long,

bitterly cold spells followed by high winds and rain. Our local everyday birds, coal tits, blue tits and great tits, appear at the bird table when conditions allow, tirelessly ferrying nuts and seeds away to some cozy den in the hedges, but I suspect that winter takes its tithes, and that the cold wipes out quite a lot of the small birds. The dunnocks, as usual, act in a frisky manner in the poplar tree; they always seem to start the mating season early. With their reputation it would not surprise me.

Ticknock, 16 January
The last three days have been dark, dull and depressing, and there was no 'pull' from the outside, and anyway I had a lot of work to do. Today, however, I headed for Ticknock for a stroll after lunch. I was surprised to find that the snow still lay on the hill, quite thickly, more than a week after the last fall. It was very pleasant to crunch along the familiar path. An eerie yellowish glow illuminated the mountains to the west, contrasting with the black of the forest fringe and the dull white of Glendhu. To the north, the Mournes, catching the low afternoon sun, were like a golden-pink mirage on the horizon, their western flanks a series of watercolour-like brushstrokes that glowed below a dark, Paine's grey sky. At the Fairy Castle I paused a while to soak up the life-giving view.

On my way downhill, I disturbed a liquid cloud of redwings foraging noisily amongst the crinkly beech leaves on the woodland floor; there must have been a hundred in the flock. They swooped up into an ash tree, and just like a Tunnicliffe painting, all perched facing the same way, feathers fluffed up. A bedraggled dunnock did a trapeze act in a pile of branches beside the track, uncharacteristically unconcerned at my proximity. It is glorious how wonderfully well one feels after forty minutes of strenuous walking, especially after the worst of the climbing is over. I arrived back at the car ten feet tall, with great swinging strides, the world at my feet!

Glendoher, 20 January
Brushing my teeth in the bathroom this morning, I glanced down into the garden to see two foxes mating on the grass under the birch tree. I raced down to get the camera, and by the time I returned they had finished the 'vigorous' stuff and were standing, bottom to bottom, tails intertwined. The female was facing me looking very relaxed, blinking contentedly, but the male was agitated. It was a case of being unable to withdraw! They remained there as I opened the window and started to take photographs, and the male, looking over his shoulder, looked at me as if to say 'Do you mind?' They stood there in this strange stance, clearly waiting for the remains of their passion to subside for a few minutes, with me clicking away, when the back door opened next door. This broke the spell: they tried to make a dash for it, but they were still connected! They ran, almost in circles, like some strange Martian eight-legged creature, for enough time for me to get off two more shots before they finally came apart, one leaping over the back wall and the other the side wall.

I've been hearing them almost every night, varying from the awful scream of the vixen to a chucking sound like birds in a bush, and I have spotted them individually around the garden and the front, but this was an unusual sight!

February

Still lie the sheltering snows, undimmed and white;
And reigns the winter's pregnant silence still...

— Helen Hunt Jackson

Glendoher, 4 February
After a seeming unending series of rather dull,
overcast days with a damp mist hanging in the
air, January morphed into February, and spring
finally arrived in Glendoher. It always begins with a
quietness. At the end of winter there is often a lull, a
calm, as nature composes herself and works behind
the scenes for the next great thrust. I wonder, was
it this quietness that led the Romans to dedicate 19
February to Tacita, the goddess of silence? There is an
acute feeling of expectation in the gardens and in the
woods and on the hills, the buds on trees and shrubs
are almost bursting with tightly vacuum-packed
herbage and ready for their big moment. During the
last weeks of winter there are occasional 'pet days',
with an hour or two of warmth borrowed from June,
as if testing is taking place, or an assurance is being
given, a 'trailer' of what is to come. I feel that if I
listen hard enough on these quiet days, I will sense
the hum of the boundless power that is being held
in check in all nature, awaiting the signal to burst
gloriously forth in colourful rebirth.

Sometimes it seems to me that it is the
widespread outbreak of birdsong that makes the first
announcement of the arrival of spring. The blackbird
that I have heard practicing on all those dark winter
mornings is now note perfect, and its mellow tunes
can also be heard in the early dusk. The song thrush
announces its arrival in the area, and becomes daily
more melodic as the days lengthen. My mother used
to tell us, as children, that if we heard a call that
sounds like 'cherry-dew, cherry-dew, cherry-dew', it
was probably a thrush.

At once a voice arose among
  The bleak twigs overhead
In a full-hearted evensong
  Of joy unlimited;
An aged thrush, frail, gaunt and small,
  in blast-beruffled plume,
Had chosen thus to fling his soul
  Upon the growing gloom.

– Thomas Hardy, 'The Darkling Thrush'

Glendoher, 6 February

Today is startlingly bright and sunny for a change, and there seem to be a lot of birds competing for the same territories. Five or six blackbirds are constantly on the go in the garden, and long-tailed tits in our Himalayan birch are almost becoming a common breakfast-time sight. Teresa saw a flock of waxwings nearby in our housing estate, and was particularly enthused about their brilliant yellow-striped tails and their crests.

I had to go into Dublin city this morning, and I walked almost a mile along the Owendoher River to reach the bus stop at Rathfarnham. Up until the end of the nineteenth century the waters of this fast-flowing mountain stream were harnessed to run many mills in the area. There was a paper mill and a linen mill at nearby Edmondstown, a mile or so south of Glendoher, and the same water that powered them continued northwards to serve another two paper mills at Newbrook and Bolton Hall, and a woollen cloth mill at Millbrook, which occupied a site just across the field from our back garden. Today, however, water mills only exist in place names, and like many small rivers, the Owendoher is ignored, which has allowed it to become a secret wilderness corridor that, shrouded with foliage, slices through the concrete and tarmac and noise of suburbia. For most of the stretch that I walked to Rathfarnham, the surface of the water was three or four metres below the pavement, curtained off from it by an old stone wall and a thick cordon of ivy-clothed trees and shrubs. Along the way, however, there are places where the wall is low, and in wintertime, with no leaves on the trees, those who are interested are afforded a view into the watery oasis. The river is lined with ash, sycamore, chestnut, oak and conifer trees, unmanaged by man, some dead and hollow, and others leaning over and trailing liana-like creepers in the rushing waters.

Today I saw that the chestnut trees are already sporting their big, sticky buds, and I noticed a couple of escapee apple trees opening delicate green and pink blossoms. Ivy is rampant along this wild corridor, where it reigns unmolested. Although hated by gardeners, it is a most valuable natural resource, providing secluded nesting locations and food for many bird species as well as habitats and late nectar for myriads of insects. It is neither parasitic nor invasive, and it takes its nourishment from its own roots, clinging to rather than penetrating the bark of trees it uses to climb to the sun. Sometimes, however, if it is not controlled, it can so weigh down elderly trees that they are vulnerable to being up-rooted by winter storms.

In places the short stretches of riverbank were covered with the pale green disks of butterbur and escapee flowers from gardens, and buddleia bushes and fuchsia, which we can expect to bloom as the year goes on, were plentiful. The birdsong along the river this morning was continuous, with chaffinches and wrens leading the chorus. Some years ago I recommended to the local authority that they build a pedestrian boardwalk along the river to allow people to access this wonderland. A small section was indeed built, but then they ran out of money and the work has not proceeded. I, for one, am glad.

Our garden at Glendoher is never without the robin's tinkling song, and the redbreast seems so much more tame at this time of year. The naturalist Richard Jefferies, in his final essay before his death in 1887, could have been talking about the robin when he wrote that 'the bird upon the tree utters the meaning of the wind – a voice of the grass and wild flower, words of the green leaf; they speak through the slender tone. Sweetness of dew, and rifts of sunshine, the dark hawthorn touched by breaths of open bud, the odour of the air, the colour of the daffodil – all that is delicious and beloved of spring-time are expressed in his song.'

It is strange that what sounds serene and beautiful to us is really, to a rival male bird, a forceful diatribe of threats, boasts and warnings. Birdsong is a multi-functional operation; it is used to attract mates, intimidate enemies, stimulate an urge to build nests and, of course, certain call notes, like the harsh click-click-click of the wren in the nearby bush, are specifically to warn of danger. The experts tell us that birdsong is controlled by the sex hormones, and is an invaluable tool in the setting up and maintaining of a territory. Singing, for a bird, actually takes the place of fighting – what a marvellous concept! When two rival birds with adjoining territories are proclaiming their supremacy, it somehow seems to be a rule that they don't sing together. When 'our' wren comes to the end of his vehement scolding song he pauses and, sure enough, his nearby rival wren, perhaps fifty metres away across the field, gets his turn to shout back!

However long the winter might seem to us today, imagine how it must have been in early times, a deeply anxious time and a matter of life and death. Family or communal stocks of food, carefully preserved and stored since the previous autumn, would have dwindled week by week, and people would daily be watching for the signs that growth would soon begin again. Some organised and long-established communities had the advantages of knowledgeable priests and great astrometric megaliths to help foresee the winter solstice, but for most, it was only the barely discernible changes in the landscape around them that might herald the return of the time of plenitude and the knowledge that they would not starve. In Ireland there were no pristine crocus petals or gleaming, drooping snowdrops to signal the approach of warmer weather, because these plants were imported from Europe much later. Spring-bringers such as the delicate white blossoms of wood anemones on sheltered woodland floors would be watched for, and, near watercourses, alders would be examined to see if their purple catkins were unfolding. The first show of the mist of tiny leaves of celandine in the soil would raise communal spirits and lead to preparations for the celebration of the feast of Imbolc, the festival of spring. The earth goddess Brigit, the exalted one, would be praised and thanked, as many centuries later, her Christian persona, St Brigid, would be similarly honoured.

For many today, those subtle signs of seasonal change go unnoticed and no longer seem to have any practical purpose. The artificial bubble that urban dwellers inhabit restricts connection with nature, for many, to their small suburban gardens, and I believe that many have grown out of the habit of 'knowing' nature. Those who work or spend leisure time in our countryside or on the hills are amongst the fortunate ones who can still be full observers, or even participants, in that wonderful transition of winter into spring. As the winds and rains and darkness of winter recede, it is a time of year that can be particularly magical for those who have the opportunity to experience it at first hand.

Kilcop, 9 February
When February arrives and the darkest days of winter are fading, Teresa and I feel a need to visit our cottage at Kilcop, which we usually close up for the winter around the beginning of November. Nearby Woodstown strand is a most peaceful place at this time of the year – the beach and seascape still and sombre, the only sounds the plaintive cries of seabirds and waders with a backing of tiny waves shuffling carpets of cockle shells. It usually takes me forty minutes to walk the beach without a halt, but today I found myself stopping frequently to watch and wonder at the great flocks of brent geese and oystercatchers quartering the mud flats. The coast of west Wexford across the harbour and Creadan Head extending out towards it from the Waterford side, were visible, barely, through a curtain of haze. Ink-

black cormorants, wings outstretched to dry after a morning's fishing, were perched on the gaunt, black poles of an ancient weir which stretches out into the tide. The sun strained to burst through the overcast and it cast a silver light on the bay, which appeared as a series of silver and grey slices, forming a backdrop to the flights of brent geese coming and going.

A dog darted away from its owners walking the beach, and created havoc as it splashed out towards the assembled flocks of gulls and waders grazing the mudflats. There was an explosion of pumping wings as varieties of gulls jostled into the air with an assortment of oystercatchers, wimbrels and geese, in the midst of which, looking incongruous, there was a lumbering grey-backed crow.

When the sky is clear, the early setting sun washes the vast expanse of Woodstown bay in a special light, reflecting off the ancient cliffs of Wexford across the way, and picking up, like tiny pinpoints, whitewashed houses scattered along the low-lying landmass. Every evening the great host of rooks that have their tree-top city in the beech trees that line the grounds of Ballyglan House launch themselves from their branches in a noisy celebration, wheeling and diving and chasing, and filling the air with a cacophony of caws.

Teresa and I had a memorable rook-related wildlife experience after a walk on Woodstown beach at dusk one evening. Creadan Head extends a couple of miles out into Waterford Harbour, and we saw a myriad of rooks gather over its northern shore, a host of black dots, and as we watched they began to stream towards us in a long line. As the flying circus of birds neared the beach on which we stood, many of them dived and skimmed across the water offshore, inches from the surface. Their calls filled the air as they swooped up fifty feet or more and headed for the abundant tall beech trees in the Ballyglan demesne. Even as the first ragged black birds wheeled and turned into the trees, the following line of birds still stretched back across to Creadan, where a circling mass of them awaited their turn in the convoy. It was an amazing sight, and we stood transfixed for about twenty minutes as the movement took place, until all the birds, with the exception of a few stragglers, lined the branches of all the leafless trees in Ballyglan, continuing their chorus of caws.

Rooks are plentiful throughout Ireland. All the better to perform the task that nature designed them for, ridding the landscape of carrion, parasites and unwanted debris of all kinds.

Kilcop, 11 February

Looking out the kitchen window today, I was surprised at how far I could see down the garden through the sparse winter foliage. I could see trees and bushes that are hidden from the window at any other month of the year. As I looked, I saw, in the midst of the grey matrix of branches, a puzzling splash of gold. I had to go out and down into the garden to find out what it was. About fifteen years ago Teresa's sister gave us a gift of a very small hazel, a tree that long ago got lost in the burgeoning shrubs and trees along the east side of the garden. It was this hazel, or more accurately, its catkins, that had caught my attention. Prompted by the sunshine of the last couple of days, the little overshadowed tree had proudly put forth its version of flowers in the form of long golden catkins, called, in some country areas, 'lamb's tails'; I think probably the first time it had produced them. In common with a number of other species of tree, the hazel is mainly pollinated by wind: when the time is right, these catkins will release clouds of yellow pollen, seeking the tiny carmine stigmas, female flowers, protruding from buds on the same or a nearby tree. The pollinated flowers develop eventually into hazelnuts with woody shells, protected by bristly bracts.

Hazel was one of the first trees to spread through Ireland after the last glacial period. Some experts believe that parts of the south of Ireland were not covered by the ice sheet and existed as an area of tundra during this time. It is possible that some hazel grew in sheltered parts of that tundra, and as the ice sheet retreated north, these hazels spread north after it. In places like the limestone-rich Burren in County Clare, hazel thrives in scrubland, and individual trees can reach heights of six metres. Largely forgotten today, in the past it was one of our most important trees. Its nuts were an important food source when man arrived in Ireland, and copious amounts of shells have frequently been found in archaeological excavations of Neolithic sites. Hazel trees were coppiced from earliest times to produce rods for making coracles, cradles, fencing and traditional baskets of every sort. Hazel rods were also used in the wattle and daub walls of houses in the early towns of Ireland, and water diviners often use forked hazel twigs. And we must not forget that St Patrick is said to have used a hazel rod to drive the snakes out of Ireland!

Kilcop, 12 February

A number of my coppiced ash trees are mature enough to harvest, and I have spent today felling them. Coppicing is a system of obtaining a regular harvest of wood; it involves felling a tree, ideally an ash, and leaving a stump about 900mm high. The mass of roots under the ground will continue to feed the stump, and so, when the growing season comes around again, the tree will put out new shoots. The ash tree produces very vigorous growth, the shoots getting up to more than a metre high in the first year. I reduce these to half a dozen shoots, allowing all the growth from the original stump to flow into the selected shoots, and after about seven years they have become a cluster of young saplings, each with a diameter of 100–125mm, ready for easy harvesting. In winter and early spring, before the sap rises, these saplings are easily felled, without having to deal with great amounts of leaves, and the process begins all over again. Today's harvest is my third here, and will provide this winter's fuel for our stoves in Kilcop and Dublin. Little coppicing is carried out today, but a careful examination of old hedges in the countryside will often reveal old, long-abandoned coppiced ash trees; they look like a half-dozen mature trees growing from the same base.

I also spent some time today working on our hedges. Bare of foliage at this time of year, individual hawthorn branches can be seen, and it is possible to access and lay some of the bushes. Laying a hedge turns it into a growing matrix of vertical and horizontal spiky branches, a living fence; it is a very ancient craft, certainly practiced since the Neolithic period. In early Christian times Irish farmers grew thick thorn hedges on the top of the banks of their ringforts, which would have been impenetrable to all but a modern tank. In attempting to lay our hedges, I am following the example of the late Tom Hayes, the man who sold the field to us. He was an old-fashioned farmer, and to pass the field out of his ownership in good order he laid all the hedges before handing it over. When I am working at laying the hawthorn and blackthorn, his labour in doing this work forty years ago is often revealed deep in the hedge, in hoary and ancient-seeming horizontal branches, a legacy of his good husbandry.

There is an art to laying hedges, as I have discovered over the years. Selected shrubs or young trees in the hedge are sliced through, near the ground, with a sloping cut, slicing in 80 per cent of the thickness of the trunk or branch. A bill hook or a hand-axe is the best tool for the job, but in recent years I have seen men use chainsaws, which the purist would certainly regard as sacrilege. The sloping cut goes through the heartwood, but leaves one side of the bush's sap-wood protected by its bark. The cut trunk or branch is then bent over: the sap continues to rise and growth therefore continues out along the branch, which will put out new vertical shoots. The end result, after a few years, is a hedge thick with thorny horizontals and verticals.

Over the years, I have planted many trees in Kilcop, and I am in awe of how fast they grow and change our little world here. Apart from being beautiful and useful, the tree is a magnificent natural engine, playing a significant role in combating erosion and moderating climate, removing carbon dioxide from the atmosphere, generating oxygen and acting as a highly efficient carbon sink. There are more than 50,000 different species of these amazing and often-ignored plants, and they are among the largest living things on our globe.

In former times, while many rural folk could obtain peat to keep them warm in wintertime, the majority relied on timber. There were severe penalties for cutting down or damaging trees, most of which had been planted by the landlord class, but the country was well clothed in rough forests and thickets, and the poor collected whatever wood and *sceachs* (bushes) they could find for their fires. This may be one of the reasons why, in the early photos of the Irish countryside dating from about the 1860s onwards, there is hardly a bush to be seen. The gathering of firewood, or *connadh*, was one of the main tasks of winter, and many illustrations of the period show old people bringing home a great bundle, called a *brossna*, of withered branches or heather for the fire.

I have learned that some species of trees are better than others for burning, and one can be guided by a poem by Honor Goodheart, 'Logs to Burn', which was printed in *Punch* magazine in October 1920 and passed on to me by my brother Tom:

> Logs to burn! Logs to burn!
> Logs to save the coal a turn!
> Here's a word to make you wise
> When you hear the woodman's cries.
>
> Beechwood fires burn bright and clear,
> Hornbeam blazes too,
> If the logs are kept a year
> To season through and through.

Oak logs will warm you well
If they're old and dry
Larch logs of pinewood smell
But sparks will fly

Pine is good, and so is yew
For warmth through wintry days
But poplar and willow too
Take long to dry and blaze.

Birch logs will burn too fast,
Alder scarce at all.
Chestnut logs are good to last
If cut in the fall.

Holly logs will burn like wax –
You should burn them green.
Elm logs like smouldering flax
No flame is seen.

Pear logs and apple logs
They will scent your room,
Cherry logs across the dogs
Smell like flowers in bloom.

But ash logs, all smooth and grey,
Burn them green or old,
Buy up all that come your way
They're worth their weight in gold.

Ash is one of Ireland's most common trees, and a good candidate to be our national tree: some of the largest and most magnificent native trees in the country are ashes – there is one on Marlfield Farm near Clonmel which is over 40 metres tall and 2.7 metres in girth. It is widely known as the wood from which hurleys are made, and the sport generates a need of over 200,000 each year. Unfortunately, less than 20 per cent of these hurleys are made in Ireland today, and so the rest have to be imported. Ash, as I have found, is also one of the best Irish firewoods, and can be burned even when freshly cut. There are many arcane uses of ash, including tapping them for sugary syrup, which can be used to make ash wine, or using the bark in a footbath as a treatment for sore feet, but in Kilcop we haven't got around to these yet.

We have, over the years, planted a variety of vegetable and fruit crops in Kilcop, but our firewood crop has been by far the most successful. I built little drying barns from waste timber and roof tiles, and it is my pleasure to stack my harvest of logs there to allow them to dry out, usually over a period of about eighteen months. So I get warm felling the trees, sawing them into logs, and finally burning them in our fire! The thinner branches and twigs, and ash have a lot of such, are gathered up and woven into the old boundary hedge, helping to make it impenetrable.

lapwing

Glendoher, 13 February

We drove back from Waterford to Glendoher
after a night during which the temperature had
plummeted, and the countryside was a magic winter
scene with every tree, bush and blade of grass frosted
brilliant white. Passing through County Carlow, we
marvelled at the flocks of lapwings that have always
been a feature of our winter journeys to and from
Waterford, although each year there seem to be
less birds. Lapwings are one of my favourites; they
look as if a mistake was made when they were being
designed and for some reason they were given the
wrong wings. They are so graceful-looking on the
ground, but when they take flight their broad and
awkward plank-like wings do not seem to belong to
their slender bodies. They nest in open ground, and
are well-known for the trick of feigning injury if you
approach their nest; they will limp and drag a wing as
if it is broken, all the while leading you away from the

nest. There is an expression in Gaelic, '*cleas an philibín*', which means 'to act the lapwing', or try to fool people. Lapwings and their eggs were highly regarded as good food in former times, and the birds were sold in large numbers at markets, and even exported from Ireland to Liverpool as late as the nineteenth century.

Hellfire Hill, 15 February
Even if it is a bit early, we enjoyed a quick trip up Hellfire Hill yesterday to see if the frogs had arrived yet for 'frog-fest', as we call it: those few days each year during which frogs come from all points of the compass to assemble at a body of water for the annual mating.

The wind, a warm blast from the south, was extremely strong and gusty; as we ascended the stretch leading to the south pond, it increased dramatically, hurling and whistling and hissing through the trees. The south pond on Hellfire Hill is spring-fed, and when I first saw it in the 1970s it measured six metres long by about nearly three wide. Long before the hill was planted in forestry in the early 1960s, when it was a farmland patchwork of stonewalled fields, the pond served to water the livestock, probably cattle and sheep. It is too small for fish, and although the newts it used to hold are long gone, it still is much frequented by frogs, particularly at spawning time. It is a wonderful tiny water world, an aquatic jungle with a community of interdependent bacteria, plants, animals and insects that have provided me with interest and entertainment for many years. I always pause at its edge, and each time, even in winter, when little stirs, I learn a little more about pond life.

Because this pond is in the open and receives plenty of sunlight, it is a particularly rich habitat, but its proximity to the forestry road used by family walkers makes it vulnerable to frog-spawn collectors and dogs having a swim. Hellfire Hill is owned by Coillte, and they frequently carry out works here, seemingly without any concern for the viability of the pond or its teeming but mostly invisible occupants. I have found, in recent years, their ecosystem's husbandry to be poor at best; with regard to this particular pond I warned Coillte years ago that it was a newt habitat, and that their works were endangering these scarce creatures, but my warnings have been ignored. There are no newts there today.

The pond water was clear yesterday, with only a wind-induced ripple to blur the underwater scene, and initially there was no sign of life. After a few minutes of careful observation, however, we spotted tiny, black, immature leeches scattered on the muddy bottom. Leeches are blood-sucking worms, of which there are 16 different species in Ireland, and 500 worldwide. Their general anatomy is much like that of an earthworm, but they have very specialised features, such as suckers to help them move, much as a caterpillar does, and an ability to attach themselves to a fish or animal and suck its blood. It is fascinating that such a small creature can have such complex parts, including a mouth that is designed to inject an anaesthetising substance so that its host is unaware that it is being 'got at' while it slits open the skin and has a meal of its blood. The leeches in the Hellfire pond in wintertime look a bit like the spines of a spruce tree lying on the bottom of the pond: at this time of the year they measure about 6–8mm long.

As I was counting the leeches on the bottom of the pond, a water beetle emerged from cover, and quickly breast-stroked across the pond from one clump of weed to another. As it did so, a sudden blast of wind nearly tossed me bodily into the water, so we left the pond behind and continued on our way. On the north side of the hill the wind was gusting powerfully, punching the trees with a great hidden fist, bending them over at impossible angles. It almost seemed, however, as if the trees were enjoying the violent molestations, revelling in swinging back to their original postures as soon the latest gust passed by.

Instead of taking the lower road past the north pond, we dropped down towards Piperstown to cut around the north-west of the hill, something we had been promising ourselves to do for some time. We found ourselves, in minutes, on a long, straight track going downhill between the trees. I once had a neighbour who professed to have great interest in, and knowledge of nature, and he asked me to take him and his two daughters up Hellfire Hill on a 'nature walk'. My son David, then six years old, came along as well. As we ascended this track, the neighbours were about five metres in front of us, chattering away animatedly and noisily and taking in very little of the surroundings through which they walked. David, who was very observant and was quick to spot things of interest on walks, nudged me and pointed up ahead. No more than six metres beyond our neighbours, a startlingly red fox had come out from the trees, and as I looked, he paused to look downhill at what was causing the disturbance. After taking in the scene, he moved leisurely across the track and into the trees on the other side; the chattering neighbours, looking everywhere but at this wild wonder, continued uphill unaware.

The secret of successfully observing wild creatures is to freeze as soon as you glimpse the bird or animal in question; stillness and silence will suggest to many creatures that, in spite of their instinctive urge to flee, you might not pose a danger to them. It is also important, on encountering a wild creature, not to look directly at it, but try to watch it out of the corner of your eye: they seem very sensitive to having eyes focussed on them.

I have found that being still can persuade squirrels that you are not a threat; if you come across one, it may escape around the back of the tree to hide out of your sight. Squirrels seem to have no patience, however; within a minute or two it will peer around the tree to see if you are still there, and if you don't move, it may assume that you are no threat, or you're gone, and will continue with its business. Stillness usually works, but the sound of a human voice can mean danger for wild animals. Walking with Teresa along the banks of a Donegal river at dawn one time, I came to a halt where a tributary flowing into the river cut off our progress. I stood there, wondering how we might cross. Suddenly, an otter surfaced across the other side of the tributary, a few metres away, water drops like diamonds dripping from its whiskers. It turned its head, and, noticing me, regarded me curiously with big bright eyes. I raised my camera very slowly, and took a couple of shots. The automatic click and wind of the camera sounded deafening to me, but it didn't disturb the otter. Instead, it swam slowly towards me. I was so excited that I called, without moving, in a stage whisper to Teresa, who was about five metres behind, to come and see. The otter might not have worried about the still shape on the bank, or the mechanical click of the camera, but the sound of the human voice rang loud some instinctive alarm bell, and the beautiful animal immediately disappeared below the surface with hardly a ripple, and we did not see it again.

On the north-west side of Hellfire Hill we saw no birds other than a solitary fieldfare; the recent cold weather has had large flocks of redwings flying over the house in the morning, maybe from their roosts in the Spinney across the field, but up on Hellfire Hill the buffeting wind kept all birds in shelter.

Glendoher, 21 February
I like February. The air is alive with promise, growth is beginning to show itself in all plants and shrubs, and the weather is reaching out towards warmth. Plants that thrive on forest floors, such as wood anemone, lesser celandine and wood sorrel, are soaking up what sunshine filters through the leafless trees;as yet no flowers have appeared, but you can almost hear them coming.

The garden at Glendoher has been mobbed with birds this spring – wrens; siskins; blue, coal, great and frequently long-tailed tits are coming to the feeder, while robins and chaffinches get the crumbs from the bird table, and the quiet dunnock weaves through the cotoneaster at the end of the garden. The dunnock may be quiet, but it is certainly not shy when it comes to mating. We watched a pair the other day, meeting up as they foraged through the garden. What we took to be the female immediately began to act like a chick wanting to be fed, stooping and fluttering her wings, while the male seemed initially a bit nonplussed, and didn't know what to do. Then he began carefully grooming the female's tail feathers with his beak. This activity must have reminded him what it was he had to do, and he dutifully hopped on her back. The consummation didn't last more than a couple of seconds, after which they both flew off in opposite directions.

Dunnocks, I have learned, both male and female, are notorious for having multiple partners. The female accepts partners other than her mate because the more males that think her progeny is theirs, the more assured she will be that her brood won't go hungry. Males have been known to have two or three female friends, simply because, I suppose, they can. They are very particular about passing on their genes, however: if a male is suspicious that a female he has chosen is 'playing away', before copulation he may use his beak to remove any other sperm from her cloaca!

Who loves not Spring's voluptuous hours,
The carnival of birds and flowers

– James Montgomery, 'The Reign of Spring'

Our friendly heron is to be seen in the garden across the field almost every morning now – and I have just found out why. The neighbours there are feeding him with, it appears, bread, actually throwing it to him, and he stalks along and takes it up. I don't think this is such a good idea.

Our little garden pond has provided us with lots of watery fun for many years now. It was created by removing the claw foot legs of an old Edwardian bath tub, and sinking it into the ground. The plughole was blocked up, and the new pond filled with water, enriched by a bucket of muck from a nearby pond and a number of aquatic plants that I brought back from County Clare. Some of these disappeared after a short while, but others have survived to this day. Around the pond we have a little 'wild' garden, a small shady place with ferns, montbretia, Solomon's seal, reeds and St Patrick's cabbage. It serves as a prep school for young frogs and other creatures before they embark on their travels in the rest of the garden. At the moment adult frogs are splashing about mating in the pond. When tidying it up last week, I was delighted to see a newt come briefly to the surface; it either came in an imported bucket of muck, or was one of a couple I rescued from a damaged pond on Hellfire Hill.

Glendoher, 22 February
There were three squirrels in the garden today at one time. They mostly ignored each other, but today one chased another around the tree a couple of times before the pursued one leapt effortlessly over the wall. One squirrel has taken a fancy to the flowers on our early-flowering camellia; we watched it as it chose a blossom and spent a while plucking petals and eating some of them.

One reason why squirrels are so bold and reckless in leaping through the trees is that if they miss their hold and fall, they sustain no injury. I have seen one fall from a height of five metres into a holly bush and scamper off as if it happens all the time, which it probably does. Every species of tree squirrel seems to be capable of a sort of rudimentary flying, or at least of making itself into a parachute so as to ease or break a fall or a leap from a great height.

Glendoher, 24 February
You don't have to go to Africa to see elaborate avian courtship behaviour. We have a pair of wood pigeons that have become regulars in the garden, partly to drink from the bird bath that Teresa has put on the shed roof, but also to take advantage of the seeds that are scattered on the grass from a bird feeder. Although they seem to be a permanent pair, the female insists each year on the male going through the usual mating procedure. It is fun to see them hopping, one after the other, doing a fluttering and flapping, leaping and landing dance, and spinning around before returning to the hopping chase. The male goes a long way to try to impress the female: he hops gallantly after her, and then does a series of deep bows, his head to the grass, his tail raised and fanned out. It is particularly amusing to watch when the female, unimpressed, just flies off, leaving the male looking around, puzzled, feeling a little daft, like a fellow refused a dance in a dance hall!

Irish wood pigeons, if they survive fledging, live for five or six years and usually stay in the same area for their lifetime. Today I was delighted to see one launch into the joyful swooping flight that characterises a wood pigeon's springtime: it flies in a series of dives and climbs, and at the top of the climbs its wings actually clap together with a slapping sound.

Glendoher, 27 February

The beautiful, delicate purple crocuses that appeared in the lawn a couple of weeks ago are almost gone now, but the daffodils are finally bursting forth and spreading their colour and warmth. For the last few days, squirrels have continued to harvest the flowers from one of our camellias. They don't eat the whole flower, but nibble some of the petals, leaving the top of the wall behind the camellia scattered with rejected petals.

This morning I looked out the window to see a pair of squirrels perching on the wall; as I watched, they started mating. I raced downstairs to get my camera, and was back with the lense out the window before they were finished. It didn't take long, but afterwards the male was solicitous towards the female, and stayed close for a while, nuzzling her, before she skipped away and down into the garden.

Hellfire Hill, 28 February

The frog-fest has been a big affair this year in our garden, with as many as seven frogs yesterday jockeying for positions in our little pond over a great heap of spawn that stands out of the water. I went up to the pond on Hellfire Hill today to see what was happening there. As the forestry road levelled out near the pond, I spotted a heron circling and alighting in a tree overlooking the water.

frog

When the bird realised someone was coming, like a vertical take-off aircraft, it extended its wings and climbed straight up, defecating two long milky squirts as it took off, and catching the wind, it banked away over the trees. Beautifully sleek and a wonderful shade of dove grey, it looked like a young bird.

The noise from the pond was startlingly loud, a chorus of 'ribbits' that sounded like a motorbike revving up a few hundred yards away. As I approached the pond, I was met with numbers of frogs apparently leaving, some males getting a piggyback ride from a female. The pond itself was alive with the creatures swimming amidst islands of spawn, the topmost globules glinting with frost in the sunlight. Many of the frogs were in great tangled lumps, slowly tumbling in the water as other wide-eyed, lust-driven males climbed aboard. I always find it an astonishing scene, no matter how often I see it. There is the deadly serious side, this vision of a delicate and vulnerable creature in a frenzy to ensure it reproduces itself, wide-eyed frenetic coupling, the male gripping the female around the throat, the latecomers grabbing on in any way they can. This mating clinch is known as amplexus, and can continue for as long as two days. It may be a fertility festival, but it has its downside; the remains of unfortunate females who haven't survived the rough and tumble are often found at the pond edge, having drowned in the act. Male frogs who haven't managed to find a female have been known to chase fish with amorous intent! One cannot help but be amused on arriving at the pond, however, at the innocent, expressionless gaze of the smaller male frogs caught clinging to a female's back or legs, crouching down and pretending not to be there.

As I watched, a raven arrived with feathers all spikey; it seemed that he had designs on the occupants of the pond, but as he tried to land, he was disconcerted by a gust of wind, and, seeing me, decided to go elsewhere.

Further on along the forestry track, wood pigeons were congregating in the trees in considerable numbers, and trumpeting their characteristic 'coo-cooooo, cu-coo' call, always reminiscent of early mornings in my childhood home in Waterford. As I walked on through the trees, the air was filled with the explosive whirring and slapping sound of the big birds bursting from their roosts above me. There certainly are a lot of them about this year; in addition to the pair that have made our garden their home, about two dozen at least are constantly hurtling to and fro around the trees in Glendoher.

March

Oh, what a dawn of day!
How the March sun feels like May!

– Robert Browning, 'A Lovers' Quarrel'

primroses

MARCH COMES IN WITH THE WELCOME
appearance in the garden of the little
brown-tailed bumblebee, buzzing around
seeking out early nectar plants. We have twenty
species of bumblebee in Ireland, but I find it difficult
to identify more than a half dozen. They are by far
our most efficient wild pollinator, and our most
numerous and perhaps our most loved insect. I say
most loved, because their slow, lazy humming buzz
is the sound of summer, and their colourful, furry
bodies are a pleasure to behold as they lumber from
flower to flower, sometimes with a heavy dusting
of nectar. Bumblebees are under threat, however:
their habitats, in the countryside and in suburban
gardens, are being seriously eroded by the expansion
of nitrogen-rich grasslands and ribbon development,
by the increased popularity of hard surfaces and
decks in gardens, and by the proliferation of flower-
less lawns. The dandelion is an early, rich source of

nectar for the bumblebee, but it is also one of the most hated 'weeds' in a garden, and rarely tolerated. We cannot do without bees, and particularly bumblebees: the only hard economic figures I have to indicate the importance of these insects are from 2008, when bee pollination generated €14.4 million of the horticultural produce in Ireland, in addition to honey sales of €992,000.

I don't believe that the population in general has realised that a global crisis is looming due to the continuing rate of extinction of our insect population. We simply cannot do without them because of their essential part in the production of the food we eat. Although the bee is perhaps one of our best-known insects, most go unnoticed by people generally. Here in Ireland, we have ninety-eight species of bee, and one-third of these are facing extinction. Our bumblebee population has declined by 15 per cent in the last five years alone, and we rely heavily on the bumblebee for pollination. This means that, if nothing changes, and we apply the same figure for every five years into the future, within forty years the bumblebee population will be less than a third of what it is today. In a global warming context, however, this situation is likely to be accelerated. These problems are being caused by the way we live today, and we need to wake up and deal with them.

Glendoher, 7 March
The birds are in full mating mode now, and I find that, if I have patience, watching their activities in the garden reveals a lot about their particular displays. The experts say that while all cock robins sing, only

about half of hen robins do so, and their song is indistinguishable from that of the cock. Why only half of them sing is a mystery to me, but this is the case; those hens that do sing usually cease when they pair with a cock.

At breakfast one March morning, I noticed a strange-looking bird in a birch in the garden. It resembled a robin with a large black spot in the centre of his breast, and held his head at a peculiar angle. When I got out the binoculars it became clearer. It was indeed a robin, which I presumed to be a male, and it was going through a courting display for another robin on a nearby branch. He had his head arched back so that the beak was pointing towards the sky, which made him look almost headless from where I stood. The stretch on the skin of his breast was such, however, that there was a large gap in his red plumage, which appeared like a black patch. As he perched in this stance, he swayed back and forth slowly, seeming to hypnotise the female, who watched him intently and curiously, head to one side. This went on for about five minutes, the male moving closer to the female twice, before they both flew off, buzzing around each other.

The cock robin draws the attention of local hens to his presence by his song, and it is after this, and sometimes weeks later, with the hen's interest aroused and with the nest completed, that the courting display take place. It is followed by coition, which is infrequent and without any display. Other than bringing the hen food offerings, the cock tends to ignore her from thereon in.

When the garden is alive with buzzing bees, flights of mallards are constantly zooming past the house and around the field, and we see our local herons flying together in close formation, spring has definitely arrived.

We have a pond-skater on our pond. He may have come in larva form with a jam jar of pond muck I brought down from Hellfire Hill to give a bit of life to the pond, or, even better, he's a descendent of the half dozen skaters I introduced last summer. Of the great diving beetles and the tadpoles I also brought, there is nothing to be seen, but what can I expect? Tadpoles are a favourite food of the diving beetle, which keeps out of sight most of the time. This mini-monster, growing to 3.5cm long, is a fierce predator, and having cleared one pond of prey, it flies on to the next seeking more victims. It has sharp jaws that bite into its prey, injecting enzymes to turn the unfortunate's insides to easily digested liquid. Even the fish are hiding at the moment, so there is little activity in the pond, other than the lone skater.

Our nearby mountain stream, the Owendoher, has not yet been fully enclosed by the foliage of the ivy-clad trees that overhang it, and I enjoy spending time on one of the little footbridges across it, waiting and watching: if I am taking the bus to town, I often leave early to allow myself ten or fifteen minutes at the river. Last week I was rewarded by the sight of, not one, but two dippers foraging along, above and in the waters, and a grey wagtail, one of our most elegant and colourful birds, bobbing its tail at the water's edge.

One of the joys of getting to know the magic of nature is to look into what seems ordinary and discover the extraordinary. The white-breasted dipper, a common enough bird on our streams, is a fascinating example of the exotic in the everyday. It's

not particularly extraordinary looking: it is a bit like
a chubby blackbird with a brilliant white bib, and
is usually seen perched on a rock in a fast-flowing
mountain stream. If it's bobbing up and down, it's
definitely a dipper, and it's from this habit that it
gets its name. While its bib and its habit of bobbing
up and down are not particularly remarkable, the
dipper's method of feeding certainly is. This bird
leaps into the water off its stony perch, and actually
walks along the bottom of the stream, swimming a
little as it hunts for a lunch of mayfly nymphs. It also
finds the larvae of the caddisfly on the bottom, and
crunching the gritty larval case in its beak, it releases
the juicy larva into its crop.

The caddisfly larva is another extraordinary
wonder of our natural world that few know about.
Caddisflies are inconspicuous browny/grey insects
that are related to moths. They also are mainly
nocturnal and feed on nectar. They have a short life,
about a month, at the end of which they lay their
eggs on vegetation near water bodies or streams.
When the eggs hatch into larvae they enter the water
and immediately begin the extraordinary task of
building a tubular shell or armoured case around
their soft bodies, a little like how a hermit crab has
to find an unoccupied shell in which to live. They
produce silken thread and use it to create the case by
assembling tiny pebbles, twigs, leaves and sand into a
tubular shape, open at both ends to allow it to feed.
Once the larva becomes a caddisfly, it cuts itself out
of its case and swims to the surface of the water, and
immediately takes to the air.

The two dippers I spotted near the bus stop were
perched on rocks that protruded from the water

(usually the rocks they habitually perch on will be marked with white guano), and every now and then, one after another, they simply ducked into the stream and vanished for a moment, before emerging and returning to their perches. It makes one wonder how these birds happened to find themselves in this particular natural niche: what is it that made them decide that, rather than have a diet of the many types of insect that can be found at the edge of a stream, and stay dry, they would swim for their food?

One cold morning a few weeks ago I was watching a dipper on the Owendoher, and was surprised to hear the bird sing. I didn't know that they sang, and this experience was a particular delight. Partly lost in the sounds of the waters rippling over the stoney river bed, the song was similar to that of the wren, a continuous lively diatribe boldly shouted from a tiny rock island.

We have four species of wagtail in Ireland, the pied, the grey, the white and the yellow. The yellow is a scarce migrant, and the white, although not uncommon, is also a migrant. The pied wagtail is the most common, the well-known 'willie wagtail', with its black and white plumage and its constantly wagging tail. The grey, however, is thought by most observers to be a yellow wagtail, because while it has a grey back and a black and white tail, it is the flash of its brilliant sulphur-yellow belly that stands out as it flies along with a dipping flight. Although it is on the list of birds that have appeared in our garden, it is almost always found near running water, where it feeds on whatever insects or snails it finds in the shallows.

Along the banks of the river I spotted a few spires of the pale purple blossoms of the butterbur, which, blooming in late winter and early spring, provide lots of nectar for early insects. The flower has a strong and sickly-sweet aroma; as soon as it dies off, it is rapidly replaced by luxuriant green heart-shaped leaves, which grew so large in warmer climates that they were used as sun hats by Greek shepherds. Statues of Mercury, the messenger of the gods, depict him wearing a hat of butterbur leaves. One of the names for the plant is pestilence-wort, alluding to its use in bringing down fevers. The seventeenth century English botanist Nicholas Culpepper said of it, 'The roots thereof are by long experience found to be very available against the plague and pestilential fevers. It were well if gentlewomen would keep the root preserved to help their poor neighbours.'

Kilcop, 3 March
Our March visits to Kilcop usually include the maintenance of the coppiced trees, cutting back any new shoots that have appeared over the winter: at this time of year even a three-week absence can find me snipping 300mm-long shoots that weren't there on my last visit.

Country living has unseen complications; in a city one's property boundaries are usually clear, but in rural areas it is not that straightforward. For the first few years we had difficulties with trespassers of various kinds. We could arrive from Dublin to find five or six goats in the field, their dung and footmarks all over the place, and they had eaten the tops of the shrubs and trees we had planted on our previous visit. They had come in from a nearby unfenced field.

One of our neighbours told us that a woman

who had moved into the area in recent times had
been seen in our field digging up primroses from
the hedge! The same woman, who owned a field
bordering our land, had trees cut down on the shared
hedge, without consultation or permission.

Initially, not wanting to start off on the wrong
foot with local people, we did nothing about these
trespasses, but this only led to more liberties being
taken, and we had to take a stand. We could not afford
to erect fences on top of the hedges that surrounded
our field to keep these intruders out, so we enquired
around and found that the goat woman lived about
a mile away. Teresa called on her and asked that she
fence her goats in, as they were doing a lot of damage
on our land. She got nothing but abuse, I'm afraid.
First the woman said she had been to confession that
very day and wouldn't tell a lie, and her goats had
not been in our field. A moment later she admitted
one goat might have been in there the previous week.
She said we would have to put up a fence around our
field, and if that was a problem, then 'the solicitors
will deal with it'!

I reckoned we would need about eighty metres
of fence posts and sheep wire to keep the goats out.
As this was beyond my budget at the time, I decided
that I would have to plant trees and shrubs in a few
distinct fenced-in copses. The destruction of the
earlier plantings was, perhaps, a blessing in disguise,
because I had naively included spruces and lawsonias
which would have caused us lots of problems later.

The goats, like their owner, have been with their
maker for many years now. One of them came to
a sticky end. The animals had been foraging in a
neighbour's garden also, and tired of wasting his time

making complaints to the goat woman, he got out his shotgun one day and fired a blast over their heads to frighten them off. Unfortunately, he aimed a little low, and killed one of the animals. The corpse had to be hidden in some deep ditch.

One March day we were fascinated to find that a pheasant had nested in our field, just yards from the front door. We all went, carefully, to look at the well-camouflaged hen sitting on her nest; the bird just sat, very still, pretending not to be there. During one of her brief absences from the nest, we saw that she had eleven eggs, ten white and one brown. We wondered about the odd one out: was a cuckoo involved?

We could watch, from the kitchen window, the hen preening herself; a beautiful sight to see as one washed up. Always vigilant, she cocked her head and gazed around every so often. Maybe she was waiting for the cock, which I had heard squawking nearby a short while before. The colourful cock did turn up the following morning, strutting in a stately way through the short grass like an Egyptian pharaoh.

I made the mistake of mentioning this in passing to my neighbour with the gun, and a couple of days later he arrived at our door with a present of the deceased cock pheasant, which he had shot 'for us'. My daughter, Fiona, in particular, was very upset that one of the beauties of our natural world, that she had enjoyed watching day after day, had been put to death for no good reason. She refused to eat the pheasant, and this incident was perhaps one of the reasons why she became a vegetarian.

In those days there were barn owls about also, and one magic night I stood at the gable of the house with my youngest son, Donal, transfixed as one coasted around and around, over our heads, with ghostly silence.

The first trees we planted in the wired off corrals were metre-high ash and beech trees dug up from the verge of the Woodstown road. When we moved into Glendoher we had planted a tree or a shrub for each member of the family in the garden; again from lack of knowledge, the one we planted for our youngest son, Donal, was a variety of Lawson cypress, but soon it became clear that it was too big for our garden. We moved this, together with an oak I had grown from an acorn and a couple of holly trees, to corrals in Kilcop, where they have thrived. When the threat of goats receded, we planted lots more beech and ash seedlings: the ashes were to become the first of my firewood crop when, much later, I learned to coppice them. I took my first harvest of ash firewood in 1996, and since then have coppiced the same trees three times.

Kilcop, 11 March
I spent the morning tidying up my roadside hedge, but not too much. I find it difficult to understand why people who build new houses in the countryside have to bulldoze their hedges and replace them with white-plastered concrete block boundary walls or white-painted timber fences. The amount of wildlife and wild plants that are destroyed by this widespread habit doesn't bear thinking about. It must be a kind of suburban mentality, the same attitude that has people turning the grass verges along the road into a linear lawn that gets mowed regularly. If one has to build in the countryside, hedges and verges should be

kept and looked after, rather than bulldozed. Modern agriculture has hounded wildflowers out of cultivated areas, and sometimes only the verges and borders of fields provide asylum for glories such as the golden discs of hawkweed, scarlet poppies, clutches of yellow vetch, knapweed, centaury and, reaching up out of them all, tall thistles, so loved by fritillary butterflies, and later on, when gone to seed, by goldfinches.

Apart from their beauty scattered colourfully through a field verge, these plants once had serious medicinal uses. Hawkweed was used to cure whooping cough and urinary complaints, and although the red poppy is called *an cailleach dhearg*, or the red witch, in Ireland, it has been used in folk medicine here as a painkiller, particularly for toothache and earache. Common vetch, a member of the pea family, was originally brought to Ireland by early farmers as fodder for livestock. The Scots had another use for it: chewing it to prevent one getting drunk during a drinking bout! Knapweed was used as a cure for jaundice, while centaury was a traditional cure for loss of appetite and a variety of stomach complaints. The thistle was believed by Pliny to provide a cure for baldness. A host of essential insects depend on these plants and flowers that grow in the verges of country roads, and the suburbanising of untold miles of verge is having a detrimental effect on them. One local observer said to me, 'why move to the country if you want to turn it into Hyacinth Bucket's Blossom Avenue'!

Kilcop, 18 March

We used to follow tradition by planting our early potatoes on this day. The soil in our field has been lying fallow for at least thirty-five years, and has, I'm certain, never been treated with artificial fertilizers. Its fecund smell, pregnant with burgeoning life, is released as one turns it with a spade. Even to a towny like me it is clear that it is remarkably rich and good; to pick out a handful of freshly dug clay and just knead it in your hand and smell its loamy sweetness is a pleasure. It has a texture that I believe they call friable, moist but granular, and it feels wonderful. A handful of soil doesn't look much, but apart from what is visible, such as worms, insects and fungi, it hides millions of minute bacteria and rhizopods, together with trace elements and other magical goodies all ready to encourage whatever plant is trusted to it. Without them, some moisture and the warmth of the sun, no plants would grow.

Experienced farmers of old would have had no problem judging the quality of a soil, although they did not fully know, in a scientific way, what it was that made a soil good or bad. To my surprise I found that it was not much more than a hundred years ago that a Hungarian called Raoul Heinrich Francé became the first scientist to reveal the myriad of microscopic riches that give soil its life-giving properties. Setting up a research institute in Munich in 1906, he commenced a scientific examination of life in the soil. He confirmed that nutrients that are removed by plants that grow in the soil must be replaced, as was done traditionally and sustainably by spreading the manure generated on the farm. As agriculture became big business, however, artificial fertilisers began to be used on a widespread basis, and they ultimately seem to exhaust the soil.

In fertiliser-free Kilcop our crops of potatoes were excellent, as long as we planted them in different places each year. We were eventually defeated, however, by the vigorous growth our soil encouraged: to keep a garden, to control the weeds and protect the crops, you must be on the spot all of the time. This is something we could not achieve, and in the past couple of years, due to projects we were working on in Dublin, we were in Kilcop less than in other years, and combined with optimum weather conditions, it was impossible to hold back nature. Our vegetable patch disappeared under a tall sward of grass and herbs, so the only crops we were able to take from Kilcop were our coppiced trees, and, in autumn, the bountiful supply of cooking apples of our one faithful apple tree. At least the insects and birds benefit from our failure.

Instead of planting potatoes this morning, I took a pleasurable stroll along a path that I have carved out around the perimeter of our garden, my tiny version of Charles Darwin's sandwalk. When Darwin moved into Down House near London with his family in 1842, he laid out a gravel path or sand walk around his land, planting hazel, alder, birch, holly and privet to delineate it. When considering intricate problems in his work, he found that walking a few laps helped him to order his ideas. Sometimes he would decide how many circuits to take, and would line up that number of flint pebbles, one of which he would strike away with his stick on each passing to remind himself how many laps he had left. Often he would pause to observe birds, animals or insects, and his son related how squirrels used to run up his legs and back.

There are no squirrels in Kilcop, but I was fascinated by the idea of Darwin's sand walk, and from our early years there I started to lay out our own version, bordered by our boundary hedge on one side, and by a row of young trees and bushes on the other. In the early days I thought it might be used by the children for a scramble-bike track, but they grew out of scramble bikes long before I got the route of the path completed, and it has not yet received its surface of gravel. It does, however, take me into the depths of our overgrown jungle, and allows me to observe nature at close quarters. In March the birdsong is continuous in the mornings – the robin, the tits, and the chaffinches producing most of the music while the big wood pigeon chips in with his 'coo-coo'. I spotted a goldcrest foraging in the top of a sitka spruce, one of a number of weed trees I brought from the Comeragh Mountains years ago to begin our tree planting, but which now have grown so big they will have to come down. Many of the trees I planted in the early years are now blocking out long views from the house and garden, and although it pains me, I have a programme of culling them before they block out our light altogether.

Kilcop, 20 March
These last couple of days the heat has brought out primroses, blossom on the plum trees, and a great swathe of blackthorn blossom in the old hedges. I have only been getting to know blackthorn in recent years, during which it has begun to proliferate in various places around the field. It seems to be

surprisingly fast-growing, and in what seems like no time at all one little seedling can become a metre-high bush. I believe that its speed of growth and the fact that a well-trained blackthorn hedge is nigh-on impossible to penetrate may have led to it being used to fortify early Irish ringforts. In one of the Irish legends, the seven sons of Queen Méabh held their enemy at bay by protecting themselves with a thick hedge of blackthorn and brambles. In ancient times blackthorn stick or shillelagh was regarded as providing protection from harm, and was carried at night to keep the fairies away, because they had a high regard for the bush. If one stick can have such power, I imagine a thick hedge of blackthorn atop the bank of a ringfort would provide considerable protection for an early farmer and his family against the little people.

Blackthorn is a very dense wood, great in a fire and, clearly, in a fight; when wielded in faction fights in the old days, it broke many a head! The white flowers of the blackthorn were a symbol of female beauty, and a Gaelic poem has the line '*Tá mo ghrá-sa mat bláth na n-airne ar an draigneán donn*', or 'My love is like the flower on the dark blackthorn'. Country people used to preserve sloes, the bitter fruit of the blackthorn, for winter use by burying them in the earth in jars, and in England, the leaves of the shrub were dried and used as 'English tea'.

Before the foliage has filled out, it is possible on my 'sand walk' to get glimpses of all the birds enjoying the spring. Today I spotted long-tailed tits and bullfinches, birds I haven't seen in Kilcop before, as well as hedge sparrows, blue tits and greenfinches flitting through the branches of the hedge, while blackbirds and wrens fill the air as usual with melody and strident whistling. For a couple of hours yesterday I had the shed door open while I was working, and during that time a robin brought in and deposited on a high shelf enough moss to fill a cornflake box, presumably to build a nest. I felt very bad about it but I had to move him on: I can't just leave the door open for the next couple of months just for his use!

March is the month that the little woodland up the road near Kilcop House rings with the busy calls of rooks building or rebuilding, all together, their little city of nests in the tops of the beeches. The rook, in its glossy black coat and grave demeanour, has a clerical look about it, so the city in the trees is like an avian seminary. They have a great community spirit, rooks, and seem always to be in conversation in the tree tops; one can imagine gossip being exchanged, disputes being settled and arguments about the position of nests taking place. It is no wonder that the group term for them is 'a parliament of rooks'.

Some birds attempt to filch sticks from a neighbour's nest, and this leads to a general hub-bub. Although their nests look like a mere stack of large twigs, they are firmly woven together, as they have to be, to withstand March winds so high in the tree. Rooks rear their young selflessly: while the female is incubating the eggs on the nest, the male keeps her fed; the naturalist Gilbert White claimed that during courtship the male rook will often replace his 'caw' with a song that borders on sweet. I have not heard this, but I have heard ravens, the cousins of the rook, use a melodious call at mating time.

In the countryside around Kilcop, at ploughing and harrowing time, rooks can be seen in the company of

seagulls following the plough, as in these lines from
'February Afternoon', written in 1916 by Edward
Thomas, a year before his death at the Battle of Arras:

> Men heard this roar of parlaying starlings, saw,
> A thousand years ago as now,
> Black rooks with white gulls following the plough
> So that the first are last until a caw
> Commands that last are first again …

Glendoher, 28 March

This morning the wind was strong and from the
west, and the vista over the top of the Spinney
was remarkable. There was a succession of huge
clouds like unending columns of great galleons,
in line astern, voyaging eastwards, with sunlit sails
ballooning. We don't look up at the sky often enough:
when it is not clear blue or dull and overcast, there
is always beauty and majesty to see there, particularly
on a windy day. It was a great summer pastime in
childhood to lie down in grass and look up into
the blue, finding clouds that looked like faces and
imagining others as strange and monstrous creatures.
It still never fails to fascinate me that these huge
bulbous things, that look so solid, have so little
substance. It only becomes clear when you fly: on
my first flight, in a Viscount to Liverpool, I spent
all my time looking out the window as we climbed
from Dublin. It was a dark, overcast day, and the
wonderment of entering the clouds and then bursting

out into the sunlight was marvellous. I was enthralled by the white, seemingly solid sea below that stretched to the horizon, and how the plane flew between great sunlit towers and occasionally through them.

April

Now 'tis Spring on wood and wold,
Early Spring that shivers with cold,
But gladdens, and gathers, day by day,
A lovelier hue, a warmer ray ...

– George Meredith, 'Invitation to the Country'

Glendoher, 1 April

It's been a very warm week, with temperatures away above average for the time of year. A high of twenty-one degrees is expected today. The sudden heat after the cold spell has brought on a rush of foliage and blossom, and has the insects and birds in a frenzy. The great beeches in the Spinney are going through their late spring sequence of colour changes: they were a dull grey a fortnight ago, but a week later the myriad branch tips had turned golden, and over the last few days, as their protective cases were shed, tiny packages of new leaves began to unfold and cover the extremities of the trees in a mist of the palest delicate green. The unfurling leaves of the beech tree are particularly beautiful, and look good enough to eat, which indeed they are, apparently. I'm told that the young leafy buds are edible raw, have a mild lemony flavour, and are good in salads. Knowing that this particular beautiful moment for the beeches will not last long, Teresa and I eat our meals in the kitchen, gazing out at them with pleasure.

In the garden, the shrub with the orange blossom, which came originally from my mother's house in Waterford, makes a bright splash of yellow in the corner between the pond and the shed, while below it Solomon's seal has suddenly produced a forest of grey-green spears from which little white bell flowers are appearing. The Japanese acer is tentatively opening its filmy purple leaves, while all around the garden the primroses, which we allow to prosper wherever they appear, are following the sun with their pale aromatic petals. Bumblebees benefit from the primrose's early blooms, and it's a favourite of the brimstone butterfly and the bee-fly, an insect that looks like a bee but has two wings rather than four.

Glendoher, 2 April

I have been carefully watching a pair of thrushes that have been active in the garden these last few days, and I'm now sure that they have a nest in the hedge at the back wall. They are extremely circumspect about entering the hedge, landing some distance from where I think the nest is, with a beak full of worms, and carefully looking around a while before heading for the nest and disappearing into the hedge. The male, or the one I think is the male, often perches a couple of metres away when the female has gone in, as if keeping a watch. When other birds approached, I saw him lower his head into his shoulders as he perched: was it to look sinister, like a small hawk?

Glendoher, 8 April

The nestlings in the thrushs' nest are now cheeping loudly when the male or female bird arrives to feed them. Between feedings, I managed to peek into the bush to see the nest, and as soon as the little creatures heard the slight rustle of the branches, a crown of cheeping beaks appeared over the top of it.

The wren, with his long and melodious but indignant call, is one of the main acts in the dawn chorus outside our window. He is accompanied by a chorus of blue tits, great tits and robins, providing the background for the blackbird's silken song, punctuated by the coo-cooing of the wood pigeons. Occasionally, passing magpie marauders drown them all out with their harsh, staccato calls. In the last few days a flush of new green has been ejecting crusty brown catkins from the golden birch, and the breeze is sweeping them neatly into the corners of the garden.

The robin is the most recognisable bird in the garden, and is always present when any work is going on that involves exposing snacks for the bird. It feeds mainly on a variety of insects and their larvae, such as beetles, moths, caterpillars, crane flies, earwigs and ants; although it may occasionally succeed in catching butterflies, it apparently does not eat them. It does eat earthworms, spiders and centipedes, and, particularly in winter, when insects are scarce, it will take small seeds and whatever fruits, such as late-developing ivy berries, are available. It doesn't have to be winter, I found, for the robin to eat fruit; one August I spotted one hovering like a humming bird in my garden, feeding on ripe raspberries.

In Kilcop one year, a juvenile robin used to turn up within minutes of me going out into the field to work. He used to perch nearby and sing, and I always got the impression that his song wasn't a kind greeting to me, but probably a proclamation, something like 'This is my human! Mine! He organises food for me every day. He's mine!'

What is not generally understood is the fact that many robins migrate, so the robin that delights you in the garden in June may not be the same bird that sings there in the winter, but might be a visitor from more northern climes.

It is difficult to believe, but robins were once caught and eaten in great numbers. In an age when things were very different to today, Baron Georges Cuvier, the nineteenth-century French naturalist, wrote that 'In France, the redbreasts are more numerous in Lorraine and Burgundy than elsewhere. They are very much sought after there, and their flesh acquired an excellent fat, which renders it a very delicate meat.' William Salmon, the seventeenth-century self-proclaimed Professor of Physick, wrote of the robin in *Seplasium: The Compleat English Physician* of 1693, 'It is good food, and its Medicinal Virtues are the same with those of the Sparrow.' The flesh of the sparrow, he claimed, is 'admirable to break the Stone and expel it, being broiled and eaten with Salt'. With other additives, it opens 'all Obstructions of the Veins, Ureters and Bladder'.

As late as 1916, in the French countryside around Toulon, 20,000 robins were killed for the table. The robin was a food delicacy not only in France but in every country, I believe, until the late nineteenth century, when the appetite for its use in food and medicine seems to have died out. Except, however, for the pious Victorians, who killed robins for their feathers, used them as trimmings for ladies' dresses, and even for the decoration of Christmas cards!

Glendoher, 9 April
Today I watched another pair of birds, blue tits this time, which seem to intend setting up home in the garden. The pair, one taking part only sporadically, seem to be clearing out a space inside the top of the hollow concrete block wall on our eastern boundary. The busy one is tireless – in it goes, only to appear a moment later with a big dried-out leaf in its beak, then it flies to the birch tree, and after pecking at the leaf, drops it to the ground, and returns to the gap in the wall to repeat the operation. Only once did I see it actually drop the 'garbage' directly over the wall, rather than flying to the birch to do it. The other bird just seemed to hover about, going in the hole a couple

of times, but not doing a great deal. The hen can lay as many as a dozen eggs, but sadly many young birds die of starvation soon after fledging. Cats are also a major cause of mortality for blue tits, and there are a few cats in the area. I love to watch these cheerful and highly active birds in their endless foraging in the garden, prying into every crevice of a tree seeking tiny insects and the eggs of aphids. Gilbert White, that tireless observer, described the bird as extremely hostile to invaders of its home, hissing like a snake and prepared to drive its sharp beak into their hand if they put it near the nest. White also described seeing blue tits tapping at a beehive, and when an angry bee comes out to investigate, the bird snaps him up.

After a period of rain, it has been gloriously sunny and quite hot these last few days. There are signs that summer is nearly here; our clematis is scattering its stars along the wall and the great apple blossom tree across the field, in bloom for a couple of weeks, is losing its blossoms in mini-snowfalls. The beeches in the Spinney are bursting into leaf, and soon we'll lose sight of the activities and battles of the birds in the topmost branches, something that has given us great breakfast table entertainment. A few days ago, as I stood in the garden, there was a lot of movement in the top branches of the Spinney. A pair of large ravens seemed to be intent on taking up residence in the trees. They dislodged a lone grey-backed crow, which circled them, moaning and groaning all the while. One of the ravens went to chase it off, and there ensued a marvellous aerial battle, the grey-backed counter-attacking, the raven doing its characteristic upside-down flip to avoid hard-pressed attacks. Eventually the pair of them disappeared off

to the south, still jinking and diving at each other.
As the other raven rested alone in the top of the tree,
a pair of magpies turned up, alighted near it, and
started their irritating 'chit, chit, chit' barracking.
The raven ignored them at first, but the magpies
moved ever closer, haranguing all the time, ignoring
the raven's irritation as it turned and honked back
at its tormentors. The magpies were persistent,
however, as they usually are, and eventually the huge
raven, who dwarfed them, was forced to leave. It flew
over my head, going south, with audible whoofing
wingbeats, honking its complaints.

Of course the appearance of what we jokingly call
the 'convulsions' in the garden is also a sign of the
approach of summer: every few years convolvulus,
a vigorous bindweed, comes in from the field,
and Teresa and I have had to form the Convulsion
Warriors to tackle it. We pull it out, dig it out, and
have to extract every single trace of the plant in the
soil in an attempt to eradicate it: we have succeeded
in previous years and are confident we can do so
again.

Ticknock, 11 April

I walked the circuit of nearby Ticknock the other day;
it was breezy, but warm enough for me to leave my
waterproof coat open and flapping. On the ascent
to the Fairy Castle, I heard the calls of a number
of birds, but the only one I positively identified
was the grouse. On the way to Two Rock, I heard a
piping call, a little like an oystercatcher, but more
of a single melodious whistle, and a flock of about a
dozen golden plover rose like a brown flying carpet

from the heather ahead of me. I had never seen them so close up before, and always thought of them as 'brown and grey' birds, but close up I could see that their markings were more intricate, particularly what seemed to be a black and white-edged breast and black beak. They wheeled in formation and settled a little farther on, only to move off again over the horizon as I walked towards them.

sundew

There is always something new awaiting you when you walk in the wild. The steady and rhythmic exercise of your limbs is enjoyable and beneficial in itself, but I find it good to use your senses of smell and hearing as a platform to heighten one's experience. I first concentrate on the upbeat, brisk rhythm of my pace, the satisfying crunch of gravel underfoot, and the swish of my boots through grass. Then I extend my aural range, like radar, to pick up other sounds: the breeze through gently waving treetops, the sweet melodious conversation of unseen, tiny birds in the foliage, the bark of a far-off dog, the cronk of a high-soaring raven.

Sometimes it is worthwhile to exercise one's sense of smell. As part of our urbanisation, we have lost so much of what must have once been a very keen sense, essential for the detection of pheromones, hazards and, indeed, food. Our olfactory sense can enrich our experience during walks in the countryside. In warm weather, when flowers are using scent to attract pollinators, the air often has an almost narcotic quality, and if you are walking in the Burren of County Clare you can be warned of the proximity of a herd of feral goats by their heavy, rancid smell! Sometimes when we are hill-walking we concentrate so much on making progress, pushing on and covering ground that we forget about our surroundings. Some years ago I wrote an article for a walking magazine with the title 'Stop, Sit, Look and Listen', dealing with the need to slow down, and indeed stop sometimes. To sit and watch a colourful beetle struggling his way up the stalk of a nearby plant, harried by ants all the way, to lazily count the varieties of herbs and grasses around, to listen to the buzzing of foraging bumblebees, the repeated calls of birds in the thickets and the almost inaudible soughing of a light breeze across the hillside, expands one's experience of nature. The poet Byron was aware of this need, and wrote of the necessity in 'Childe Harold':

> To sit on rocks, to muse o'er flood and fell,
> To slowly trace the forest's shady scene …

On the way back down from Ticknock, I looked in a particular place for the delicate green leaves of the butterwort, and sure enough, as always, I found them in their usual marshy habitat, with a few ready to produce their flower in a week or two. Years ago, on a May morning on Carlingford Mountain in County Louth, I came across a cluster of these tiny plants, with pale-green, pointed leaves in a rosette, each with a single stalk supporting a delicate purple flower, but I could not identify them. On returning home I consulted my wildflower books, poring over many photographic illustrations to try to identify what I had found, without success. I finally turned to an old, much-treasured book, Fitch and Smith's *Illustrations of British Flora*, which contains wood engravings, like pen and ink drawings, of almost every plant that grows in these islands. In a short time I found a clear image of what I had seen: its name was the common butterwort, one of our very few insectivorous plants, and, for me at least, a very thought-provoking organism. In the mists of time, this plant found that it could not get sufficient nutrition in the soil in which it grew. Somehow, whether through mutation or some other magical process, it developed, over time, the facility to seek sources of nutrition other than those from the earth by trapping passing insects and absorbing from them what it needed. The leaves are covered with a combination of two fluids, one thick and sticky, a little like the fly-paper of old which traps small insects, the other an acid digestive fluid, similar to what we have in our own stomachs. The leaf closes around the hapless trapped insect, the digestive fluid gets to work, and within hours there is nothing left but the 'hard bits', scales, wings and claws.

There is a story attached to my copy of *Illustrations of British Flora*. It contains over 1,300 black and white line drawings of plants, and I had bought it for a pound, years ago, at a jumble sale. While all the wood engravings in the book were in black and white, some, including the butterwort, had been delicately tinted with water colours. A penned note under the coloured illustration of the butterwort stated that the book's owner had come across the plant 'near Carlingford, Co. Louth, on the 25th May 1927'. Clearly she had painted the illustration too. The front flyleaf indicates that the book was a gift to Annette J. Spence, 'from her loving pupil, Iris H.H. Ainsworth, on 9 August, 1926'. It looked as if Annette had retired in the summer of 1926: the volume was lovingly bound with stitched canvas for use out-of-doors, and it seems that for the next few years, as Annette explored the countryside around Dublin, she lovingly and delicately coloured in the line drawings of plants she had found. Under each little masterpiece she noted where and when she had found it. Only a small proportion of the plants in the book are so coloured, and the last 'entry' noted is the water dropwort which she found beside the canal near Castleknock on 31 July 1928. I often wondered what became of Annette and her love of wildflowers, seemingly enjoyed for such a short time. Her pupil, Iris, was easier to track, with the help of Doctor Google. She was aged ten in 1926; her father and mother had divorced the previous year, and within months both had married again. In 1926 Iris went to live with her mother and stepfather, Hans Wellesley Hamilton, 2nd Baron HolmPatrick, in Abbottstown House in Castleknock, County Dublin, where the James Connolly Hospital now stands. Since that Carlingford day, as I wander in perfumed boreens, I am still reminded of Annette and Iris.

Botany is the most accessible of all the sciences to ordinary people. No matter where we are in this world, we are surrounded by plants of all kinds. It is a thought-provoking subject; every plant we see, even down to the most prosaic of common weeds, is a success story. For countless thousands of years they have continued to flower, seed and multiply. Occasionally, like the butterwort, they have had to change the way they grow, feed and broadcast seed to stay alive in altering, and sometimes radically changing, climatic conditions. Weeds, in particular, are true survivors. Not only have they had to deal with the natural ecology around them, but since the arrival of the human farmer, they have had to resist deliberate attempts to eradicate them. Not all plants have the necessary tools to survive; the fossil record is full of the ghosts of plants that thrived for many thousands of years, only to eventually become extinct.

Glendoher, 15 April

A few days ago, passing the garden pond, there was a flurry in the water, and leaning in to see what had caused it, I was delighted to see a newt hovering at the surface, and then diving for cover. I wondered if it was the one I had spotted earlier in the year. Newts live for up to fifteen years, so it could easily be one of the original pair of smooth newts that I 'rescued' years ago from a pond on Hellfire Hill that was being damaged by forestry workers. Newts are rarely seen because they are nocturnal and they spend much of their lives in dark cool areas, such as under logs, rocks or compost heaps, frequenting ponds only during the breeding season. The animal

common newts

has a sticky tongue which it uses to catch its prey, and
it will eat tadpoles, worms, slugs, snails and spiders.
They are notoriously bad, however, at judging the
size of suitable prey, and are often seen attempting to
consume creatures almost larger than themselves.

Ireland has only three species of amphibian:
the frog, the natterjack toad and the smooth newt.
Newts are under threat of extinction, particularly
because of what seems to be a lack of knowledge of
biosustainability among the decision-making staff in
bodies such as Coillte, Ireland's largest landowner.
Although responsible for the natural environment of
the area around Hellfire Hill, many of the operations
that Coillte carries out in association with harvesting
timber do not take into account important natural
features such as ponds. The pond in question had
been almost destroyed and drained away on a number
of occasions by forestry machinery, until the newts in
the pond at spawning time had been reduced to two.
It was these two that I took, with the idea that they

had a better chance of continuing their species in my garden pond. So far, so good.

I really must start looking down more and concentrate a little on the micro-natural world, which is teeming with interesting creatures and happenings. Under every stone in the garden is a gathering of creatures sheltering from the heat of the sun and the attention of predators. The first thing that one of my grandsons, Sam, does when he goes into the garden is have a look under an ornamental Buddha to see if the woodlice are still there, and if he is in luck, there might be a fast-moving, glistening brown centipede darting this way and that, or a shiny black beetle. This morning, looking down rather than up, I found, beside the garden pond, a dragonfly larva half-metamorphosed into a dragonfly. The old grey/brown larval case seemed far too small for the creature that was emerging from it. The process of extricating itself was very slow until I moved the case into the sun, and then within ten minutes the dragonfly was out and staggering about. It had a striped 15mm-long body and an iridescent green head with frog-like bulbous eyes. Its wings were just little stumps, but after about an hour they were fully extended, glistening gossamer, trembling and gleaming in the sun. A half-hour later he was gone.

When I look at a dragonfly, especially up close, I have to pause, very deliberately, and clear my mind, because this creature is a link to a far and distant past, the prehistoric world before the advent of man. In spite of a sense that this was a 'primitive' period, dragonflies are highly complex creatures, intricately engineered to allow them to fly manoeuvres that no aircraft could. In the fossil record they date back

350 million years, and have changed little physically, although some early examples had wingspans of 750mm. Dragonflies are predatory insects, and the combination of their phenomenal eyesight and their astonishing power and agility in flight means that few midges, mosquitos, butterflies or moths can escape them. Even in their larval state, in water, they will prey on anything that is not bigger than themselves, including other insect larvae, tadpoles and small fish. I don't see many dragonflies around Glendoher, but I do see plenty of these examples of 'super-nature' in Kilcop in summertime, and am pleased that this is one insect that doesn't seem to have reduced in numbers in recent years.

Glendoher, 18 April

In the past two weeks foliage has smothered the trees, and the perfumes in the garden are wonderful. An iris bulb we brought back from the Pyrenees, which flowered for the first time last year, has six fabulous purple blossoms this year.

Teresa saw a raptor fly low and fast through the garden yesterday with a mouse in its beak – it could possibly have been a merlin. Today there was a flurry of beating wings and panic calls from birds in the back garden while I was having lunch, and I looked out to see a large brown bird land in one of the conifers in the field. To get a good view, I ran upstairs, and indeed, there was a large raptor, one of our Spinney sparrowhawks, a female, perched on the top of the tree. She stayed there for a few minutes, but must have realised that the element of surprise was gone, and she went off to hunt elsewhere. We have never seen house sparrows in all our years here in Glendoher, and I wonder is it because of our resident sparrowhawks?

For the first time in many years, starlings have appeared again in Glendoher. I like their cocky manner and their busyness, and it's good to see them back. They used to live in the roof barge board, which they accessed through a hole in the rotting timber, but since then, we have had new PVC fascias fitted, so they went elsewhere.

Kilcop, 20 April
From the beginning of spring we try to spend as many weekends as possible at our cottage at Kilcop,

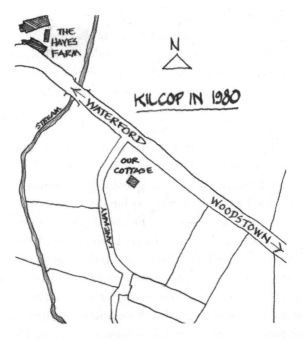

Kilcop 1980

County Waterford. The area has changed a lot over the decades, and nine houses have been built in the surrounding fields over the years. At this time of year, before the sound-insulating foliage of our trees and shrubs has filled out, the air is full of the sounds of lawnmowers, dogs barking and kids playing in the gardens of the houses around. The neighbours we have met are warm and friendly, and always helpful when we have a problem.

Our own little arboreal enclave is as peaceful as ever. The grassy area around our cottage could not be termed a 'lawn', although, for simplicity, I have called it such on occasions. More correctly, it is the original meadow that was here when we bought the

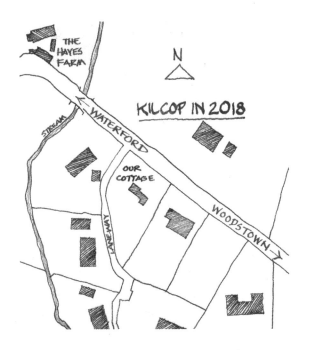

Kilcop 2018

place, periodically tamed, and planted with trees and shrubs. It contains many if not all the plants that co-existed with the grass in those days. One is the plantain, which raises its black flower head in midsummer. The club-like top on the stalk gave us, as children, great enjoyment playing conkers. The plantain has been part of agricultural meadows since Neolithic times: core samples taken down through two metres of bog in the Wicklow Mountains have revealed the spores of plantain, allowing archaeologists to surmise that these upland areas were farmed five thousand years ago, before the bog began to grow. Its palatable leaves and seeds provide valuable nutrition for grazing animals. In former days the leaves of the plantain, or *slánlus*, plucked and chewed, were regarded as a good dressing for a fresh wound, preventing blood poisoning and encouraging healing. I'd say one would have to be careful about who did the chewing.

Birdsfoot trefoil is another meadow plant that adorns our grass. Apart from its beauty, it is the reason we see lots of tiny common blue butterflies in summertime; it provides nectar for this butterfly and food for its caterpillar.

Another plant that we have in our grass, and not as welcome as the previous two, is rough hawksbit, with its dandelion-like yellow flower. A few years ago it began to spread, and I had to deal with it by digging out many plants. It has a deep tap root that sustains it through droughts, but makes it impossible to eradicate by simply removing the plant above ground.

When we built the cottage, we got a High Mac to dig a hole eighteen feet deep, and into it we put two four-foot-diameter concrete pipes on end. We fed the hose from the pump with its filter into the pipes, and carefully filled them with rounded cobbles from the beach at Woodstown, topped with a few concrete slabs covered with earth. Gradually the ground water seeped into this sump, and it was this that we used for all washing purposes. For a number of years, however, our only source of fresh drinking water came from the local well, which had been in use by the people of the neighbourhood for more than a century. It was in a field a couple of hundred metres up the road; a little gateway in the hedge led to stone steps which brought you down into a wildflower-perfumed glade. In the middle of the glade stood the little well, sheltered by an arched roof and closed off to animals by a tiny iron gate. The water was crystal clear and always cool and refreshing.

We had a two-gallon plastic drum with a tap attachment, and the children used to go down to the well to top it up regularly, such was the relative safety of the roads in those days. After a couple of years, we had to cease using the well when we found that a farmer had started to use it to clean out his milk churns. We were probably the last people to use it for our drinking water: by then, most houses around had their own drilled wells. We made enquiries about the possibility of a group water scheme for the area being organised, but we had no success, so we arranged to get a well drilled. The contractor positioned the complex-looking equipment in our driveway and drilled down 180 feet in half an hour, through limestone, at which level artesian water was found. A steel tube was inserted in sections, leaving only the installation of the connecting tubing and the pump to complete our water connection. It cost us £400. Two weeks later a community group called on us to say that a new group water scheme was going ahead, providing water piped to each house, and did we want to join?

Kilcop, 24 April

The sunsets here in Kilcop have been very beautiful, and at most times over the last two days the blue-grey undulations of the Comeragh Mountains have been visible to the west. I have been exploring the Comeraghs since my father used to take us climbing there when I was a child, and it is a great thrill to glimpse them from east Waterford. The mornings have been mild and misty with sun breaking gloriously through from time to time. For my sixtieth birthday, my children bought me a covered timber garden seat, a kind of tiny gazebo, and I love to sit out there in the morning, drinking my breakfast tea while butterflies flit about my head and hover flies and bees buzz about, to and fro. Early this morning, while I was drinking a morning cup of tea, I heard an early cuckoo deep in the valley through which a stream meanders. We saw our first swallows this week, and the earthen banks of the hedges are laden with posies of primroses. At the bottom of the field, near the gable of an old stone shed, I found an interesting hybrid flower. It had a cowslip stalk, with the usual spread of flowers at the top, except the flowers are like primroses. Coloured slightly yellower than the adjacent primroses, the flowers also seemed slightly smaller. Later I found that this hybrid is not uncommon, and is called the oxlip. It's always wonderful to be finding new things in nature and learning a little more.

The Spinney at Glendoher

Rabbit spoor in snow

A snowy day at the Fairy Castle

Aerial battle over the Spinney

A Glendoher fox, taking the sun

Airing barns at Kilcop

Brent geese at Woodstown

A squirrel tucking
into a camelia
blossom

Frogfest in our pond

'The flower on the dark blackthorn'

Wren proclaiming in Glendoher

Glendoher garden

Dragonfly

The oxlip I found near the old stone shed in Kilcop

The gleaming beach at Woodstown

The stonechat on Hellfire Hill

My mother showed me that even common wildflowers, dare I say weeds, have a wealth of history behind them. Who would have thought, for instance, that the dandelion, named from the French *dent de lion* recalling the golden teeth of the heraldic lion, was richly praised by many seventeenth- and eighteenth-century poets, that its roots were used by poor peasants in Germany as a substitute for coffee, and that it is a proven medicinal remedy for liver complaints? Even the little daisy that suburban gardeners abhor in their lawns was Chaucer's favourite flower, and had its unique uses. It was said to encourage pleasant dreams of loved and absent ones when placed under the pillow and to provide a readily available salve for soldiers' wounds on the battlefield. In the days of chivalry the little daisy, much maligned by lawn-keepers, was a symbol of romance: a knight had a daisy tattooed on his arm to signal to all that he was in love. Another unpopular plant for gardeners, ivy, is known to have been used for romantic spells, particularly one that a young woman would use to try to see what lover she would find:

> Nine Ivy leaves I put beneath my head
> To dream of the living rather than the dead,
> To dream of the man that I will wed,
> And see him at night at the foot of my bed.

Ivy was also seen as an effective protective agent against witches, and to protect livestock from diseases ivy garlands might be placed on entrance doors to animal sheds. It had many medicinal uses, such as, in poultice form, a treatment for corns, and children suffering from eczema might wear a cap of ivy to combat the condition.

In old times when plants were being used for medicinal purposes or indeed for spells, their accurate identification was particularly important. While I no longer have my mother to name the unfamiliar plants I find, there are plenty of books showing myriad species in perfect, sharp images, and, of course, there is little that you cannot find on the World Wide Web. While I never became an expert on botany, with my mother at my shoulder I have always remained a devotee, and have found endless pleasure during walks in the countryside discovering species that were new to me, and later seeking to identify them and searching for what folklore had to say about them.

Kilcop, 25 April

The night sky at Kilcop is still quite dark, in spite of the increase of houses in the area, and we are always fascinated by the starlit firmament. At this time of the year the night sky is so different from later when we regularly spend time star-gazing. I was at a loss for a while last night to find the most recognisable star grouping, the Great Bear, or Plough. Then I spotted it, over the house, upside down – it will obviously rotate around the North Star to its more familiar position before July.

On our early morning walk along the gleaming beach at Woodstown, we were delighted to see that the sand martins are back in force along the cliffs at

the northern end of the beach. I counted twenty-
four nests in one area, and the martins cannot have
been here for long, because some birds were still
excavating their tunnel nests. About a third of the
size of swallows and house martins, sand martins
are such tiny and delicate creatures; they are almost
like butterflies as they flit around. They winter in
central and west Africa, and so these tiny birds that
are darting along Woodstown beach have crossed
the Sahara Desert on their way here. And in a few
months, with their eight-week-old progeny, they will
line up on the barbed wire fence atop the cliff until
it is time to go, to fly across thousands of miles of
land and sea to a warmer clime, or find death along
the way. Walter de la Mare summed up the martins'
departure thus in 'Martins: September':

> Each preened and sleeked an arrowlike wing
> Then eager throats with lapsing cries
> Praising whatever fate might bring –
> Cold wave, or Africa's paradise.

May

Queen of months, supremely fair,
Cloth'd with garments rich and rare,
None in beauty can compare
With thee, sweet May.

– Peter Burn, 'Ode to May'

honeysuckle

Glendoher, 4 May

Today I bought two speckled goldfish called
shubunkins, and introduced them to our small
garden pond. They immediately disappeared into
the darkness at the bottom. I've been told I will not
have to feed them if there is plenty of weed in the
pond, and so I have added extra plants brought down
from the pond on Hellfire Hill. I have been assured
that one is female and the other male, although I
cannot figure out how one can tell. The two fish have
different markings, and even though we don't know
which is male and which is female, Teresa has named
them Flossie and Fred.

We have had a robin's nest in the shed for the past
few weeks. There were five eggs, and they seemed to
take ages to hatch. For a while before I discovered
the nest, I was puzzled: almost every time I opened
the door and walked in, there would be a panicked
flapping sound and a robin would dodge by me and

out through the door. How did it get in there? I wondered. This happened a few times, until I noticed bits of dried leaves and twigs on my workbench. Glancing up, I saw what appeared to be a handful of leaves tucked into a shelf high over the workbench. There are all kinds of things in my shed that I have collected on my wanderings in the countryside, from sculptural bits of wood to interesting stones, from an old sheep shears to dried plants. For a moment I wondered if this was something I had brought home and forgotten about, until I realised it was a bird's nest. And indeed, there were five little speckled eggs in it.

By careful observation, I discovered that the robin was gaining entry to the shed by way of the gap under the door, and as soon as the baby birds worked their way out of their shells, the two parents were locked into constant feeding. I had to stay out of the shed because was afraid I would disturb the process: as a child I was told that if one touches a bird's nest, one leaves a trace that will force the parent birds to abandon the nest and its occupants. The two birds would not enter the shed unless I sat quietly opposite it, and then they would deign to hop along to the door and disappear under it. One by one, the young ones fledged, and when I had to enter the shed there would be a flurry as those out of the nest would fly to a high point and observe me curiously. Also one by one, these juveniles were shown the way out of the shed, and once out from under the door, they disappeared into the shrubs. We could hear them in the undergrowth for a while after, cheeping to be fed. It took a week or so to clear the nest, and then all was quiet in the shed, and I was back in ownership.

I learned two things from this experience. First, I could find no traces of egg shells, so I have learned that either the parent birds or the young eat the shells, presumably to boost their calcium levels. I also learned that the volume of droppings produced by five young robins is prodigious; there wasn't a thing in the shed that had not received their blessing.

Like some other birds, adult robins moult in July and August, during which time they are rarely heard because they hide away; I like to think that they are embarrassed, perhaps, about their looks. They return to their normal habitats by September, and the autumn is spent with the males singing and fighting and re-establishing defined territories. Hen robins also sing, but not all of them, and their song is the same as that of the cock. After pairing with a male, they tend to keep quiet. By late December and January there is an upsurge of male song. Although many juvenile robins die before reaching adulthood, and even adults do not survive hard winters and predators for more than a few years, there are records suggesting that, in favourable surroundings, the bird is capable of living for up to a dozen years.

Kilcop, 8 May
In the beginning, our tiny cottage at Kilcop looked naked, and it stood isolated in the field for a number of years. We used to call it 'The Little House on the Prairie'. From the very beginning, I wanted to populate the field with shrubs and trees, and, in some way, recreate the garden that I enjoyed as a child in the Waterford suburbs. Our family home was built in the grounds of an old house, and my father had

to carve a garden out of an extensive, overgrown and chaotic shrubbery. After he had cut out, around the house, small terraced lawns, an apple orchard and a vegetable patch, he left what remained to us children, as a kind of wilderness playground. It consisted of a hillock covered with a variety of species of shrub and tree, from mountain ash to a grisilinia bush that had grown into a large tree, from bamboos to mature laurels. We named it 'The Jungle', and it provided play opportunities of all sorts for me, my siblings and friends.

After the goat problem had been solved in Kilcop, we began to plant trees and shrubs around the cottage. It soon became clear, however, that, as absentees, we could not properly maintain the whole acre, so we divided it in half, fencing off a meadow to the east, which we eventually sold. We divided, with a new hedge, the remaining half-acre into a cottage quarter and a vegetable garden and orchard quarter. I love hedges, but took a lot of time and effort to create this new one. I didn't want a straight, manicured hedge, but rather an informal one of mixed species. We first planted a curving row of pyrocantha, an expensive shrub, but one that has been very successful in Glendoher. Its flowers provide nectar for the bees, its thorny interior is ideal for nesting and its pretty red berries provide autumn food for the birds. I mixed in with the pyrocantha a few berberis, some variegated grisilinia, a dozen escalonia and a couple of native hawthorns. I finally added a shrub that I'd bought at a garden sale and which I thought was a hydrangea. To my surprise, however, it turned out to be a magnificent *Viburnum plicatum Mariesii*, examples of which I saw a few months later, in their true glory,

when we visited Loseley Castle in Surrey in England.
It produces, in early summer, a veritable froth of
lacy white flowers, and remains perhaps the finest,
and certainly the most aristocratic, shrub we have in
Kilcop. When I trim the hedge now, the viburnum
alone is allowed to spread its delights whatever way it
desires.

Our 'new' hedge looked pathetic for quite a while
and took nearly twenty years to reach a point when it
could honestly be called a hedge. Behind it we planted
an upper storey of lilac, forsythia, and a 'golden glow'
buddleia. The buddleia, in particular, has given great
enjoyment, its golden, globe-like blooms assuring
us in late summer of plenty of butterflies. At night
the shrub attracts lots of moths, less in recent times,
but they in turn attract preying bats, and I have
stood close to it in the dark with insects and animals
buzzing around my head. As evidence of our lack of
knowledge about trees and shrubs other than those
we have known since childhood, we also planted a
small robinia and, at considerable expense, an *Acacia
purpurea*, a beautiful small tree with feathery foliage.
Neither lasted a year.

The hedge is now forty shades of green, and
I allow the shrubs a lot of freedom, trimming a
curvaceous top so, with its sinuous curves, it looks
a bit like a seaweed-draped sea monster swimming
across the lawn. The hedge varies in thickness from a
metre to two metres, and I'm sure that it now houses
a population of small birds and insects.

Sitting reading in the quiet of an afternoon, I
can hear a sound like someone pacing slowly and
rhythmically through dried leaves – it's a blackbird, of

course, head swinging back and forth methodically, rummaging with his yellow beak for insectivorous delights.

When my mother was in hospital in Dublin in the autumn of 1987, my sister Olivia came over from the United States to see her. I took Olivia for a walk one day in St Enda's Park, near our home in Glendoher. The climate that year had been unusual in terms of rain and sunshine, and it was one of the rare years when Irish sweet chestnut, or Spanish chestnut trees, brought forth viable nuts. I took three from the ground under a chestnut tree in St Enda's and planted them in pots. One of them came on well, and was eventually planted in Kilcop, in the north-east corner near the hedge. In spite of the sycamores in the hedge overshadowing it, the tree came on well, and today it is nearly six metres tall. We have dubbed it 'Mother's Hospital Tree'.

There is another Spanish chestnut tree in Kilcop, grown from a nut that Teresa and I brought back from travels. In 2008 we walked a section of the Spanish Camino to Santiago de Compostela. It was the month of October, and many sections of the route were carpeted with the prickly nut cases from the many chestnut trees that overhung the path. I took a few home and, again, one grew well and now stands in the middle of the field, four metres high, as a living momento of our camino. The sweet chestnut is a Mediterranean species, and is thought to have been introduced to Britain by the Romans, who favoured it for its nuts as well as its wood.

Woodstown, 10 May

We found today that the beach at Woodstown was strewn with the bulbous remains of barrel jellyfish. It is a phenomenon that happens every few years and today we counted up to thirty of the stranded creatures. *Rhizostoma octopus* is the largest jellyfish normally found in Irish waters, and it can grow up to 900mm in diameter and weigh as much as 40kg. The biggest we came across today was about 600mm in diameter. While most jellyfish last only one summer, these monsters can survive for three or more seasons. Their sting is not harmful to humans, and they have been called the 'basking shark' of jellyfish: they feed only on tiny plankton. I still wouldn't like to come across one when I'm taking a swim.

Unlike many beaches, the idyllic Woodstown I knew as a child in the late 1940s and early 1950s survived intact until about a decade ago, when major changes in the nature of the beach began to happen. At the northern end, at least a metre and a half of sand has been stripped off the beach over the last decade, revealing bedrock and a glacial till of cemented cobbles. It was formerly possible to drive down to this northern end of the beach, which was always less crowded, and we did this many times, taking our children for swims. This lowering of the level of the beach has exposed the bottom of the fifteen-metre-high boulder clay cliffs at the back of the beach to high tides, and they are being severely eroded; I calculate that more than a linear five metres has been lost of the fields on top of the cliffs in the last decade.

When I was a child, among the millions of cockle shells that gave the beach its whiteness, one would find many razor clam shells, some as long as 250mm, and all of them useful in our sandcastle constructions. These are almost completely absent from the beach today, their place taken by oyster shells, escapees from the oyster farm offshore.

One of the only shortcomings Woodstown used to have of old was an annual build-up of seaweed at the southern end in about July every year. I presume this was weed that grew on the rocks along the headlands that mark the southern end of the beach and was annually stripped from the rocks in bad weather. This phenomenon has somehow now expanded in the last few years to affect almost the entire mile-long beach.

When I remark on these changes to local people, some say, 'Well, that's global warming for you!' while others suggest that the extensive oyster farming offshore might have something to do with it.

Sometimes as we walk Woodstown beach after rough weather, we come across mysteries of the past. Soft sandy coastlines change constantly, being moulded this way and that by tides, winds and high seas. Sometimes the tides clear the beach sand off boulder clay beds that are normally hidden far under the beach. These Woodstown beds are hard, like the rock the Victorians called 'pudding stone', but although the stones and rocks in it are well cemented in, it hasn't yet become bedrock. Along the beach we have found, on occasion, clues of geological magic: stretches of dense, black clay with the prominent remains of tree trunks, branches and roots projecting from it. The tree remains look just like the debris on a forest floor, broken branches lying this way and that as if smashed down, but with lots of roots in section, as if the top 300mm or so of the tree has been removed by the sea. To add to the mystery, recent excavations to construct a new drainage chamber on the beach nearby exposed a layer of peat a metre or so below the level at which the trees lie. I collected some of it and, after drying out, it burned reasonably well in our stove. We often find ourselves standing on the shore trying to fathom these mysteries that provide us with a window on to a world that existed here many millennia ago. It was not difficult, for instance, to close one's eyes and imagine oneself standing in a dark forest of pine trees, through which ran herds of wild boar, while stately red deer grazed the grass in sunny clearings and wolves watched from the shadows.

The geological record for this part of Waterford Harbour suggests that the peat dates from 38,000 years ago, but it is not clear when the trees in the drowned forest grew.

When I was a child, at the first sign of mild weather we had family expeditions to Bluebell Valley, an old beech wood perched on the northern side of a wooded headland south of Woodstown. It is anything but a valley, but somehow the name became adopted by our family. Our expeditions involved following the narrow paths that wended their way out through the beech trees, and included a brilliant view of Woodstown strand and bay stretching off into the distance to the north. In springtime and early summer, the slopes under the trees were a mist of delicate powder blue, and along the way during our walks we would pick bunches of bluebells for our little May altar. They were the first wildflowers I can remember noticing; Keats so well described the plant as 'Sapphire queen of the mid-May'. Another flower of those days was the delicate primrose, which was known as the herald of spring because they were the earliest blooms to appear in abundance after the long Irish winter.

thrush

Glendoher Road and Hellfire Hill, 15 May

After a few days of awful, dark, drizzling weather, the sun came out on Thursday and banished the damp and the drear. It was a brilliant day for getting out, and, promising myself to work late instead, I slipped away in the afternoon and climbed Hellfire Hill, taking the long way around the hill. At the far side, I heard a cuckoo nearby, in what trees remained after the devastating clear-felling of March. He was so close that I could, or sensed I could, hear the sound of his breath in the making of the 'coo-coo' note. I worked my way quietly along the trees searching for a glimpse of the bird, and was rewarded for my stealth: there he was, the characteristic back-pointing wings and tail, giving of his best. As I moved to get a better view, he spotted me and flew away. Farther along the path I heard him again, from down the slope of the harvested forest. As I stood listening, he flew directly towards me and landed in a tree only fifteen metres away. He sang a few notes again, but I think then sensed my presence and flew back the way he had come.

The following morning I went up again, armed this time with binoculars and camera. Along the northern boundary of Coillte lands, I came to the attention of a pair of stonechats. They kept coming close to me, perching on fence posts and gorse sprigs, calling in an agitated manner. The female had a tuft of horsehair in her beak, and I wondered if I had disturbed them building a late nest. I made the best of their proximity with the camera, and then started downhill again. They kept pace with me, scolding me, until I must have passed the unseen boundary of their territory – they were clearly satisfied I was going away from their nest, and they sat a few minutes longer, calling after me, before returning up the hill, presumably to their nest.

The long promenade up along the northern side of the hill offered up nothing more than a rabbit scurrying across the track, and I was disappointed as I reached the west corner that there were no cuckoo calls.

A picturesque log pile had sat on the roadside since the harvesting in March, and I took a photograph of it with Kippure Mountain forming a backdrop. As I did so, I noticed, perched on one of the projecting logs, a nest woven with twigs and upholstered with green moss. A bird's beak projected out of one side, and the feathers of a tail projected from the other. The bird made no move as I drew closer, and I saw that it was a thrush. What a ridiculous place for a nest, I thought, with little or no shelter from the rain, right beside the forest road and in full view of all who passed by. I reminded myself, however, that I had passed this way the previous day and had not noticed the nest.

After a pause of a few days, I revisited the nest. When I was a good distance away, the thrush flew past me, and when I got to the nest I saw that it was occupied by four beautiful eggs, pale greeny blue with brown speckles. I was still certain that she had built her nest in the wrong place, and it would come to a sad end. A week later I went back and watched the male and female thrush coming and going from the nest, feeding their hungry offspring. When both were gone, I had a close look. There were four chicks now, and when my shadow fell on them they all opened their huge beaks and squeaked for food. These vigorous young organisms were astonishing: I could see right down their gaping throats into their bellies.

I was still concerned for their safety: when I returned a week later, the nest was empty. I hope it was because the young had fledged and flown happily away.

Glendoher, 21 May

The sky over Glendoher today was busy with criss-crossing, squealing swifts. I am sure the recent heavy rain and the heat of the sunshine of this morning would have brought millions of flying insects into being, and it was this bonanza that the swifts were enjoying. If the density of insects in the air twenty metres up is the same as at ground level, however, they have to work particularly hard to get a meal, but I suspect that there are many more up at that height to be hoovered up.

There was more rain forecast for later, so I walked over to St Enda's Park for a circuit or two before the rain came again. There is a lot of evidence to show that urban residents have considerably more pleasant places to walk and take the air than rural people, and it is not unusual today to see rural people getting their exercise along the sides of busy roads. Dubliners enjoy the amenities of a number of large estates and gardens developed by the well-off over the last couple of centuries, and St Enda's, within walking distance of our home, is one such park. The other is the larger Marlay Park, a little farther away. I find that if I go early in the morning to either of these, I have them almost to myself, as if they are parts of my very own estate.

Today the growth was at its full, early best, still fresh, fragrant and new, and a long way from late summer when foliage becomes jaded and a little oppressive. A light fresh breeze had deposited a varied and colourful carpet of arboreal flowers on the paths of St Enda's, which were as yet untrampled, reminding me of the flowers that the faithful strew before Corpus Christi processions in Madeira.

It is easy to forget that almost all the great trees produce flowers, often copiously, but usually their displays are seen on a grand scale, and it is rare enough to get the opportunity to examine individual blooms. Today, in particular, I enjoyed examining a single blossom from a pink chestnut, a tree that always reminds me of Paris, and which provides one of the most beautiful displays at this time of year. Almost hidden within its delicate rose-pink flower, its petals have a glorious flame-like orange base, and its stamens have red tops like matchsticks; it is this combination that gives the effect of the tree such punch.

Glendoher, 28 May

I'm pretty sure now that the bird I've seen twice in the last week or two in the garden is a merlin, perhaps the same one Teresa spotted in mid-April. The first time the bird crossed the garden very fast at low level, and only a glimpse of shape and speed suggested it was a raptor. A couple of days ago, however, I caught sight of it emerging out of the side passage and gliding low at great speed across the garden, before jinking neatly between trees and heading across the field to the Spinney, with prey hanging below it in its claws.

June

A delight the season:
Winter's harsh winds have gone;
The woodland is bright, the water fruitful,
Peace is great, summer is a joy.

– ninth-century Gaelic poem

Glendoher, 4 June

The day dawned bright with glorious sunshine. Summer is here at last! In the garden a wren was feeding three demanding and manic young, one after the other, as they chased her along the cotoneaster and around into the flowerbeds. Where this wren has her nest I do not know, but it must be somewhere nearby. Wordsworth is not a favourite poet of mine, but sometimes his lines appeal to me, such as the following from 'A Wren's Nest':

> Among the dwellings framed by birds
> In field or forest with nice care,
> Is none that with the little Wrens
> In snugness may compare.
>
> No door the tenement requires,
> And seldom needs a laboured roof;
> Yet is it to the fiercest sun
> Impervious, and storm-proof.
>
> So warm, so beautiful withal,
> In perfect fitness for its aim,
> That to the Kind by special grace
> Their instinct surely came.

The wren is, surprisingly, the second most widespread bird in Ireland after the meadow pipit, but, when I think about it, I realise that I have seen or heard wrens in every corner of Ireland, from my garden to the high mountains.

Flossie and Fred, the two shubunkin goldfish
I bought a few weeks ago, are chasing each other
around and leaping almost out of the water to get
a good bite of the pond weed I brought down from
the Hellfire pond. They seem to be settling in, and
I've seen them chasing the waterboatmen that must
have been imported with the weed. I've put some
rocks into the pond to provide a 'hide' for the fish, in
case our local heron comes looking for them. These
little insects are designed to cruise around, just like
a rowing boat, and graze on algae and pond plants,
and their four long rear legs are shaped like oars to
aid their swimming. Only one pond skater remains
of the little crowd that used to populate the pond.
Although no doubt lonely, he has the potential food
supply all to himself, and is clearly very well fed on
the mites and flies that find themselves marooned on
the pond's surface. This insect is an amazing creature:
its body and limbs are covered with micro hairs, more
than one thousand per millimetre, which allows it
to actually walk on water, and provides resistance to
splashes or rain drops. I was surprised to learn that
many of them have wings and can fly, which might
explain the disappearance of the rest of them from
the pond.

Magpies are criss-crossing the field, their harsh
rattling calls almost drowning out the house martin's
twitterings and the squeaks of the young wrens.
Mother wren is clearly very anxious about her brood.
The wren's call is the loudest and most insistent of all
the garden birds, and it is easy to believe that, in spite
of its tiny feathery frame, this creature is convinced
that it is the 'king of all birds'. It feeds on insects

and loves soft, fat spiders: its long and sharp pointed beak leaves no prisoners in the dead vegetation of the garden. Long before my mother pointed out the little 'cock of the walk' to me at the kitchen window in my childhood home, the 'wran' was known to me in song. We were always awoken on St Stephen's Day morning by a bunch of lads from Wilkin Street, where poor families lived in tiny cottages. They gathered outside our front door and sang, with great gusto:

> The wran, the wran, the king of all birds,
> St Stephen's Day got caught in the furze,
> Up with the kettle and down with the pan,
> Give us a penny to bury the wran.

Then, if there was no movement in the house, they would add a musical plea:

> Mrs So-and-so is a good woman,
> Is a good woman, is a good woman,
> Mrs So-and-so is a good woman,
> She always gives us something!

In old times, the poor wren was blamed for betraying St Stephen, the first Christian martyr, and in the old days the tiny bird would have been caught and killed, mounted on a stick and paraded around the houses. By the time I heard the song, in the early 1950s, this part of the tradition had, thankfully, died out.

Glendoher, 5 June
This morning I harvested compost from both of our composters, filling a large tub with dark, rich-looking

clay. We began composting about a decade ago, starting with one composter, a large polythene bin without a bottom, sitting on a patch of earth at the side of the house. We were amazed at how light our garbage bins that we put out for collection by the local council became, and how fast the materials we put into the composter were reduced down. All organic material can be composted, so we fill our composter with potato and vegetable peelings, banana skins, egg boxes, grass clippings, some newspapers and some leaves. These are processed by a range of different organisms; although earthworms are the most visibly obvious creatures at work when one looks in, they are assisted by insects, fungi and millions of soil bacteriums. Oxygen is also needed, so we aerate the collected material regularly with a garden fork. The result is a dense, soil-like stuff that we use to spread on the garden to feed our plants. I only need to harvest compost about four times a year, and still find it amazing that everything we put in can be reduced to so little.

There are few areas in our back garden that are not now showing the blue petals of the forget-me-not, a wild flower that has become a favourite of those who prefer a garden that looks after itself. The flower is a symbol of love in European folklore, probably derived from the story of the knight who falls to his death in a river, but, remarkably, has the time to throw a bunch of the flowers to his lover, calling out 'forget me not'! I suspect, however, that the name comes from the fact that this self-seeding plant is extremely difficult to get rid of, if one wishes to do so, and it keeps reappearing. The wild plant is found in damp places, and its petals seem to me to be smaller than those of the domesticated flower. My forget-me-nots are descendants of those that grew in the garden of my parents' first house in Waterford in the 1940s, then served their time in their next house before coming north and following us through two Dublin locations; they are as vigorous as ever in our Glendoher garden. The plant is also known by the very different name, Scorpion Grass.

London pride is another plant now in bloom in our garden, its tiny pink and white flowers held up on pink stalks. It followed the same journey as our forget-me-nots. With its delicate flowers and shiny serrated leaves, it was one of my mother's favourites, and she was surprised when I told her that I had found it in high places in the MacGillycuddy Reeks. This wild variety is called St Patrick's cabbage, but it also has another name with Irish connotations, 'Prattling Parnell'; what the connection with Ireland's uncrowned king is, I do not know.

Ticknock, 7 June

Today dawned muggy with a low ceiling, and the trees of the Spinney were reduced to grey shapes in the mist. In the garden I was astonished by the number of spiders' webs of all sizes and shapes, made visible in the foliage by tiny droplets of mist. It is clear that there are many more spiders active in the garden than I would have imagined. I read somewhere that one spider can eat as many as 2,000 insects in a year, including the aphids, leafhoppers, beetles and caterpillars that feed on plants we have sown. Based on this, it would seem that the occupants of the webs that were visible to me would deal with more than a quarter of a million insects each year!

After my spider experience in the garden I slipped off for a walk up Ticknock. I hadn't been for a while, and now the pale and delicate green of new growth had covered the hills all round, and they seemed to glow in today's unusual light. To the east the view was very dramatic, a series of mother-of-pearl washes where the hidden sun lit up the Irish Sea. I stopped and sat a while on the stone cairn on the Fairy Castle summit. Out over the sea it was clear of mist or cloud, and the Welsh mountaintops lined the eastern horizon, with Holyhead Island and Snowdon standing out like volcanic islands in a silver sea. The Fairy Castle is now, perhaps, since the installation of good gravel and stone access paths, the most popular of the Dublin foothill summits, and the ancient cairn on top is rarely without walkers admiring the views. The fact that upland Wales is clearly visible from here means that Neolithic inhabitants of that place would have been able to see Ireland, with the green of the forests that covered the land at that time highlighted by the morning sun. Some of them were clearly drawn, in good summer weather, to take on the voyage across the Irish Sea to this emerald isle, bringing with them new farming practices and livestock. Their ancestors, indeed, may have built the cairn, which provides a high throne for me, to commemorate their dead.

Another strand of thought this morning made it difficult for me to sit on the summit and not to imagine what this place was like even further back than the time of the cairn builders. During the last glaciation, great ice sheets, more than a kilometre thick, moved southwards from the Scottish Highlands. Along the way, these mobile ice mountains tore blocks off the bedrock they passed over, scooped up mud, shells and sands from the bed of the Irish Sea and transported it southwards. I have found polished pebbles of a beautiful, pink granite on Killiney beach that are what remains of rocks scraped off the island of Ailsa Craig that lies sixteen kilometres off the mainland of Scotland. Ailsa is also known as 'Paddy's Milestone', referring to its being roughly halfway between Ireland and Scotland on the route that so many emigrants from the North took. On top of this Dublin foothill, 536m above today's sea level, fragments of sea shells and layers of gravel can be found that once, many thousands of years ago, lay on the bottom of the north Irish Sea. I am fascinated by such ideas: they are just another aspect of our natural world, one that puts everything around us today, and particularly man's short-lived occupation of the landscape, into startling perspective.

I always have to drag myself away from places like the Fairy Castle, which fire the imagination, and I started off downhill. A squealing call from the sky caused me to look up, and I saw two buzzards circling above. As I watched, a pair of passing rooks took it into their head to have a go at the buzzards, and they began to subject one of them to diving attacks. The buzzard simply jinked and dodged them, without altering too much its graceful circular flight. The rooks made another few attempts to spoil the buzzard's morning, but their attentions were half-hearted, and soon they continued on their way. It is the same with all raptors; every other bird species, from large to tiny, will do their best to chase off any raptor that appears. It struck me that I should look up and scan the sky more often in the mountains: if it wasn't for the birds calling, I would have missed this avian activity.

On my way down, I noticed that the larch trees on the hillside had shed the husks of this year's new clusters of cones, and that the ground beneath the trees was carpeted with shiny, crispy golden-brown sheddings that look like some new honey-coated breakfast cereal.

Glendoher, 13 June

I'm sitting out in the warm back garden at 10.20 p.m., and it's still bright enough to write. Our local bats are doing their usual circuit of the field, a preliminary to extending their hunt out of our sight. They seem to have grown in confidence in the past month since their first appearances this year; their wing-beats are less frenetic and they are flying more like the swifts in whose company they hunt their food in the gloaming. I used to think that bats do not glide, but I have learned that they do, in short stretches, and are capable of doing intricate manoeuvres and direction changes while gliding. Ireland has seven species of bat, but I rarely get close enough to them to be able to guess at what species I am looking. I suppose those I see in the evenings over the field here are pipistrelles. Although it is only about 4cm long, the delicate wings of the pipistrelle have a span of about 21cm. It weighs no more than a one euro coin, but can consume as many as 3,000 midges and mosquitos in one night, which they detect using their astonishing echo-locating abilities. The bats that take to the air in Glendoher probably come from the Spinney, or the Owendoher River cordon, where they roost in holes in trees.

One of the most exciting natural history events I ever experienced involved bats, and it took place near a town called Fredericksburg in Texas. My Texan nephew Tony drove us about ten miles from the town through wild prairies to visit a disused railway tunnel, where Mexican free-tail bats had taken up residence. There was a Texas wildlife ranger's post there to protect the bats and to provide 'interpretative services'. We arrived well before twilight, and descended a rustic stair into a valley to sit, with about twenty others, in a glade overlooking the tunnel mouth. An elderly warden explained the ecological niche that Texas bats occupied; this particular nesting place had a population of 1.6 million bats, who, every night during the summer, harvested 14 tons of moths from the surrounding countryside. The caterpillar of these moths is extremely harmful to agricultural crops, so the bats save the farming community a fortune in insecticides, and also from the downstream pollution that such insecticides would cause. As he talked, three great hawks glided into view high over the tunnel mouth. Looking up at them, the ranger commented that they were red-tailed hawks, and seemed a little early, but usually they came about five minutes before the bats flew, so it wouldn't be long now.

Not a lot more than five minutes passed before a few stray bats appeared, circling around the tunnel mouth before heading out across the trees for the open country. Then there were more, and then more again, as the glade was filled with the sound of tiny wings beating the air, and a mild stench of bat guano was blown from the tunnel by the numbers now coming out. They swirled around in one great oval, as if getting their collective bearings, and then spiralled in a stream upwards and out between a gap in the trees. There was a continuous flow of tiny grey beings, a flickering river that grew thicker and thicker in that looping spiral that poured skywards.

Up in the sky more hawks had arrived and, with squealing calls to one another, they plummeted down into the river of bats in an evening feeding frenzy. Still the flood of bats continued to gush out of the tunnel, and the looping circuit they followed expanded slightly as the numbers increased, until the outer edge of the rushing river was passing within metres of our faces, and we could feel the breeze.

For twenty minutes this astonishing river of bats flowed on, and then it began to slowly dry up, until the last stragglers went darting after the pack. We left our seats and climbed up to the top again, from where we had a good view out over the countryside, and, although we could see the bats no more, we could see the hawks continuing to wheel and dive as they continued their hunt far into the distance.

Glendoher, 16 June

The great tits are feeding their young along the garden wall – the youngsters are olive-greenish on the back and wings, more colourful than their parents. The blackbird is trilling away; how is it that we become so used to the beauty of his song that we hardly hear him anymore? The blackbird's song is

perhaps the finest we have: one ornithologist who
was also a musician described how she was amazed to
hear a blackbird, from simple beginnings, 'compose'
a phrase almost identical to the opening phrase of the
rondo in Beethoven's *Violin Concerto* (da daa da da da,
da daa da da da, da daa, da daa, da da da da daa!).

I watched a blackbird on a budding sycamore
One Easter Day, when sap was stirring the
    twigs to the core;
I saw his tongue, and crocus-coloured bill
Parting and closing as he turned his trill;
Then he flew down, seized on a stem of hay,
And upped to where his building scheme was
    under way,
As if so sure a nest were never shaped on spray.

– Thomas Hardy, 'I Watched a Blackbird'

Glendoher, 17 June
We have had yet another balmy evening that
encouraged me to sit out until late. I love to watch
the sky and its strings of wispy cloud as it gets dark,
and watch our visitors from thousands of miles to the
south, swallows, swifts and even a few house martins,
revel in their evening meal of juicy Irish insects. The
swifts can be identified in the air by their scythe-
shaped wings and their graceful and 'swift' flight: they
are one of the fastest birds you will see in Ireland.
Their 'srriiii' squeals in the evening time also mark
them out, but I find that they don't use that call as
much here as I have heard them do in Mediterranean
locations. The swift is a remarkable bird, and they say

that, other than when it makes nests and lays its eggs, it never lands, and normally eats, drinks and mates on the wing. In her poem 'Swifts' Anne Stevenson described the birds and their flutter:

> Quick flutter, a scimitar upsweep, out of
>   danger of touch, for
> Earth is forbidden to them, water's forbidden
>   to them,
> All air and fire, little owlish ascetics, they
>   outfly storms,
> They rush to the pillars of altitude, the thermal
>   fountains.

They have tiny short feet that are suitable only for gripping a vertical surface, and they make their nests in sheltered crevices or cracks high up in the walls of buildings. I found a young swift on the ground one time at Killaloe Cathedral, which must have fallen from a nest. It was dragging itself pathetically along the ground with its wings, unable to take to the air. This beautiful, warm, downy creature stayed still as I picked it up, and when I gently cast it into the air it flew vigorously away. Swifts winter in the tropics, and come to Ireland for their summer holidays between May and September.

Kilcop, 20 June

We usually spend the month of July in our little cottage in County Waterford, but this year we have managed to escape to the country early. A soothing peacefulness descends on me as soon as we pass through the Kilcop gateway. I can remember times when my architectural practice in Dublin was quite stressful, and being amazed with myself for being able to just sit out on what we called 'the stoop' for long periods, doing nothing other than watching the sky, the trees and the birds while I slowed down to the pace of the countryside. Kilcop is close not only to Woodstown, but also to many beaches and coves that are strung along the nearby coast, while for more energetic leisure activities the Comeragh Mountains are not far away to the west.

When I take my mug of tea out into the garden early in the morning and sit into my little gazebo, I enjoy looking out across the many shrubs and trees, where a few decades ago there was nothing but meadow grass. This morning, while I was still in sleepy mode, lulled by the gentle swishing of breeze-blown foliage, my mind wandered into a subject that has always fascinated me: 'What was here before?'

Geologists are divided on the matter, but some of them believe that this triangle of land between the Atlantic and Waterford Harbour, what is called today Gaultier, was, like a large slice of counties Waterford, Cork and Kerry, not covered by the ice sheet that clothed Ireland during the last glaciation. It may have been the first part of this island to be colonised by Mesolithic peoples from the east and south about 10,000 years ago. Nobody knows this for sure, but advances in paleoarchaeology will no doubt, within a few decades, fill in the gaps in knowledge about the distant past. Possibly thousands of years before this, the tundra landscape would have been inhabited by arctic hares and other fauna, possibly stoats, which would have fed on both the hares and fish. Long before the rest of Ireland began to be colonised by

vegetation, Gaultier was already covered with a dwarf
wildwood of juniper and hazel and many plants and
herbs. Small familial groups of human, fur-clad
hunter-gatherers would have had a good life here
for a few millennia, towards the end of which some
of them found that clearing ground and sowing, in
an organised way, some of the wild plants they used,
vastly increased their food supply and security. This
radical change in their way of life laid the foundations
for the agricultural land use that has characterised
Gaultier ever since. While the phenomenon of man
taking control of the landscape had little initial effect
on the flora of the region, there would have been
a gradual loss of much of the post-glacial fauna,
while some, such as wild pigs, would have survived
as domesticated animals. Bears were here, but big
animals like this could not last long against human
co-operative hunting, and so they were driven into
extinction. Otters survived, as did pygmy shrews and
stoats, and in time they would have been joined by
wolves, badgers, foxes, red squirrels and deer, which
were probably brought to Ireland by human pioneers.
There were, of course, from the beginning, birds, but
the archaeological record includes remains of only
larger birds such as duck, pigeon and eagles, so we are
not aware of which of our modern birds were about
in those days.

Kilcop, 23 June
At this time of the year Kilcop is full of life.
Goldfinches are in the field and I have watched them
feeding on grass seed and plantains, twittering as
they fly in short spurts overhead. The far-off call of

a buzzard is frequently heard, a call that has become
familiar over the last few years, and high up in
the clear blue I spotted two of them this morning,
circling in a thermal at about two thousand feet.
They were soon joined by another, and the three of
them continued to circle and call to one another – a
wonderful sight. They climbed considerably higher
as they drifted south-west and were soon out of sight.
Buzzards are relatively new to Kilcop, but some birds,
such as the yellowhammer, once common, are long
gone. We used to have one in the south-east corner
of the field singing repeatedly through the spring
and summer, 'a little bit of bread and butter and no
cheeeeeeese'. It was my sister Olivia, who has a great
ear for birdsong, that identified his song for me and
sent me down to try to spot him. Creeping slowly
along the hedge, I finally spotted the little beauty, atop
an elder bush, giving its best in an attempt to attract a
suitable mate and get on with the job of nest building.
It reminded me of John Clare's 'The Yellowhammer':

> Dead grass, horse hair, and downy-headed bents
> Tied to dead thistles – she doth well provide,
> Close to a hill of ants where cowslips bloom
> And shed o'er meadows far their sweet perfume.
> In early spring, when winds blow chilly cold,
> The yellowhammer, trailing grass, will come
> To fix a place, and choose an early home,
> With yellow breast and head of solid gold.

The chiffchaff turns up in Kilcop every summer, and
its 'chiff-chaff' call echoes through the trees all day

long. It's a member of the warbler family, but an odd one out in that clan in that, rather than a melodious song, it repeats, over and over, its name, and so is easy to identify. Even having identified his call, I find it difficult, as with all warblers, to spot the bird itself, which has an unremarkable 'brownish' colour, with a lighter-coloured breast. This little bird's travels are anything but unremarkable: it flies here every summer from southern Europe and as far as North Africa, and spreads throughout all parts of Ireland, except, strangely, north Mayo. In the heat of a Kilcop summer, its song is a constant, while the wood pigeon makes his sombre speech periodically, 'coo coo, cuck coo coo, coo coo, cuck coo', and ends it with a full-stop 'cuck'. The wren is another bird with an unmistakable song – its indignant tirade comes from deep inside my hedge, or from a high branch. The blue tit's comments are familiar, and it's clear that the rooks in a nearby tree have difficult progeny that are always complaining loudly and the poor parents don't seem to know what to do. Occasionally, a pheasant's harsh squawk cuts through from a nearby field.

Kilcop, 29 June
The wonderful combination of meadowsweet and purple spires of loosestrife are beginning to decorate the roadside ditches here, earlier than usual. The meadowsweet is a valuable food plant for bees, butterflies, moths and hover flies, and traditionally it had many medicinal uses. It has a strong perfume, although a little too sickly sweet for my taste, and the old books say that it can cause 'violent headaches'! It seems, however, that in ancient times the flowers

and the leaves were used to decorate houses and banqueting halls in summertime, and the leaves used to be put into claret to give it a 'fine relish'. In the days when threshed meadow grass was used as a temporary floor finish in houses, meadowsweet was also scattered. Thinking about this, it dawned on me what the original meaning of the common term 'threshold' was: a bar, in stone or timber, at the external doorway that 'held' the 'thresh' from flowing out of the building. The Irish name for meadowsweet is, oddly, *Lus Cuchulainn*, or 'Cuchulainn's weed', because the superhero used it in his bath to soothe his rage. Is there a commercial possibility here?

In spite of the fact that purple loosestrife's Irish name, *créachtach*, means 'wound herb', I could find no records of it being used for healing wounds, but it was used to treat diarrhoea. This plant is widespread throughout Ireland, except, strangely, according to the botanical maps of the Botanical Society of Britain and Ireland, in the province of Ulster. I would dearly love to have these two plants in Kilcop, but until I take the matter in hand and transfer some from a roadside verge, I will have to make do with great stands of rosebay willow herb that have taken up a place beside our old pump house. This tall, pink-flowered plant's Irish name is *Lus na Tine*, or fireweed, because it is one of the first plants to appear after a fire has passed over land. It can look unsightly when it goes to seed because of the downy fur that eventually take the seed on an aerial journey.

Another plant that is beginning to appear now, filling some fallow fields and waste ground with dazzling gold, daisy-like flowers is the ragwort. There is one place along the cliffs outside Dunmore East

ragwort

where it dominates, and the combination of golden
ragwort, emerald sea and blue sky there is an artist's
delight. It is a great food crop for many insects and,
indeed, to see a flock of goldfinches quartering an
area of ragwort when it is in seed in the late summer
is a glorious sight. The foliage of ragwort, however,
is toxic to livestock; I remember when the law laid
down that landowners were obliged to remove it from
their land or suffer prosecution, but, like a lot of
these countryside laws, they seem no longer to be of
interest to the gardaí.

In Irish mythology the fairies used ragwort as an
otherworld horse to ride upon to abduct young female
humans at Halloween. It is also called the Herb of St
James, whose feast day is 25 July, when the plant is
fully in bloom in Ireland. St James, apart from other
heavenly responsibilities, is the patron saint of horses.
I wonder is there a connection with the fairies here?

July

Blue July, bright July,
Month of storms and gorgeous blue;
Violet lightnings o'er the sky,
Heavy falls of drenching dew …

– Unknown

Kilcop, 4 July

Yesterday I was amazed to see a pair of pheasants
courting outside my bedroom window. It was a bit late
in the year, and it seems the hen thought so too. The
cock performed gallantly by jumping in front of the
hen, bowing and fluffing his feathers like a peacock.
The hen just ignored him and walked on, so he had
to jump in front of her again and repeat his dance.
She eventually tired of it all and flew up into a tree by
the road, and after a few attempts from the ground,
the cock gave up and stalked off. He was like a reveller
in a Venetian masque, his hooked beak protruding
like a white nose from a shocking red face mask, and
exaggerated black ears sticking out on each side of his
head. It was a strutting walk, a proud and dignified
withdrawal, but I could imagine his mutterings.

Yesterday I discovered a wild beehive in a hollow
tree down in the corner of Gobbo's Garden. A local
man who had been keeping bees in a nearby field
passed away this year, and I thought that maybe these
had escaped. I should explain that Gobbo's Garden is
in the southern extremity of Kilcop, bordered by the
old boundary hedge to the west and a shrubbery of
blackthorn to the east. The level of the ground here
is lower than the rest of Kilcop, and so I have been
'filling' it over the years with grass cut from the lawn,
rubble of any kind, unchoppable tree trunks, clumps
of weeds and the sweepings of the driveway; to date I
have emptied over 200 barrowloads there. Because
we are occasional residents in Kilcop, we have no bin
collection, and I have also used Gobbo's Garden to
deposit obsolete things such as a toaster, a radiator, a
toilet seat, a vacuum cleaner and a broken chair until
there is enough for a trip to the recycling centre. One

of our grandchildren discovered these, set them out and called it Gobbo's house, after a naughty goblin in a Noddy story. All the grandchildren delight in the place, and the area of fill has become known as Gobbo's Garden.

This evening, as the sun set behind the tall aspen next door, the swallow family that nest in a nearby shed returned after their day out, circling and dipping and full of song, as if joyfully chatting about their day. After a while they were joined by more families, like a twittering, social bedtime gathering overhead, and I counted up to three dozen birds before they finally settled into their roosts.

I never tire of sitting out and watching the gloaming descend, and last night, again, I watched the world going to sleep. The poet Shelley writes, in 'A Summer Evening Churchyard':

> Silence and Twilight, unbeloved of men,
> Creep hand in hand from yon obscurest glen.

I love the silence and twilight and indeed, how

> They breathe their spells towards the departing day,
> Encompassing the earth, air, stars, and sea ...

A pure gold aeroplane passed over at 30,000 feet, highlighted by the sun which set some time ago. An app on my phone told me it was an A380 that had left Abu Dhabi thirteen hours before, and had a further six hours to go to reach its destination in Boston,

Massachusetts. Washes of pink cloud were draped across the sky, and one greyish cloud in the midst of it all disappeared slowly over a matter of a few minutes – it was amazing to watch it just de-materialise. As the evening closed in, a blackbird chuck-chucked quietly in the bushes, and a wood pigeon clattered about in one of the big ash trees. The rooks were returning in dribs and drabs to their roosts in the trees at Kilcop House, and a robin, no doubt the one that keeps me company when I'm cutting grass, kek-keked down in the apple trees.

In spite of the lack of moths that I have noticed in recent summers, I was very happy to see that there are still a few bats about. During one of my evening sit-outs I saw three in short order, two flying together. Although I always feel, from their panicky style of flight, that they are not entirely convinced that they should be in the air at all, bats are in fact expert aviators. They can change direction far faster than a swift or a swallow, which makes them more lethal to insects. Changing direction is usually achieved, whether by a bird or an aircraft, by using an adjusting tail, but bats have no tail, so they have to carry out these often-complex manoeuvres entirely by using their wings.

Kilcop, 8 July

Walking the Dunmore cliffs today we saw two seals along the foam-fringed rocks, near the picturesque cove of Portally. They are not common along these cliffs but I know a woman who has, on a number of occasions, swum with seals in the sea at Portally. It is a good lobster-fishing coast here, and I suspect

common seal

fishermen discourage seals from looting their pots by
shooting them from time to time.

Great tufts of yellow vetch and cushions of slightly
withered thrift were shivering in the breeze, and
copper-coloured soldier beetles are using the frothy
domes of wild carrot for mass mating. They are slow-
moving creatures, not soldier-like in the slightest,
and, as I found out as a child, harmless and easy to
pick up, in spite of their other name, bloodsuckers.
While this slowness must make them vulnerable,
their colour perhaps warns potential predators that
they carry toxic defensive chemicals. Soldier beetles
feed on aphids, pollen and nectar, and have a short
life; they are commonly seen at this time of year, tail
to tail, mating, which used to amuse me greatly as a
child.

Teresa and I have been walking the cliff path
here for many years, and not long ago, when it was
established as an official pathway, I had the honour to
be asked to perform the opening ceremony. Although
a short walk, about four kilometres to Portally Cove
and back, for picturesque surroundings and drama,

it equals any coastal walk I have ever done. The route
follows fractured old red sandstone cliffs westwards
to the narrow heather-and-thyme-clothed Portally
Cove, and the views across the broad Waterford
Harbour to where the ancient Hook Lighthouse
reaches into the gleaming and limitless Atlantic
are particularly fine. Hester Cooke, a local poet,
described the cove in 'Portally', which concludes:

> Oh, tired feet a-tramping city pavements,
> Ah, weary hearts that find no rest each day,
> Could you but know the peace and splendour,
> Abiding now around Portally Bay.

I have never walked the cliff path without meeting at
least one family of choughs roller-coasting along the
cliff edge and calling 'kai, kia, kia' to one another.
They are a joy to watch. The chough is a crow, but
a crow with a difference, sporting carmine legs and
a long, pointed carmine beak, and it is to be found
only in landscapes where artificial fertiliser is not
used. Unlike the usual statistics regarding British and
Irish birds, we have the vast majority of choughs in
these islands, mainly on the south and west coasts.

Kilcop, 10 July

Because of our long absences, I spend much of the
early summer in Kilcop beating back burgeoning
nature from submerging the driveway and the cottage.
After a week of work, I'm beginning to see the light
at the end of the tunnel: it's a battle against brambles
and weeds this year. I'm afraid that the great crops
of raspberries and strawberries we once enjoyed are

a thing of the past; the vigorous growth of the early summer grass and the blackbirds, which ignore my most elaborate scarecrows, reduced our harvests considerably. The few ripe raspberries that they leave are not enough to harvest for desserts, but they do provide me with delicious treats as I pass by. A single ripe raspberry is a flavour bomb in the mouth, and fills me with a strong remembrance of childhood summers.

Any plant or shrub that grows too big for our garden at Glendoher is retired to Kilcop. A few years ago, when one of our sons was moving into a new house, he planted a garden, and had three bamboo bushes and two small conifers left over. I was happy to take them, particularly the bamboos, which were an important part of the 'jungle' we were blessed to have in my childhood garden. All five of these are doing very well in Kilcop, although I am now aware that the bamboos will have to be carefully controlled; apart from putting up strong and tall new canes, the most amazing suckers, or spreading roots, radiate underground for many metres from the main plants, producing a new plant above ground every metre or so. It is easy to see how, in the rich soil of Kilcop, bamboo could easily take over.

Kilcop, 12 July

Our plum trees have provided good harvests in the past, but they are becoming swamped by the jungle. Looking out the kitchen window the other morning I saw what appeared to be a squirrel in the nearest plum tree. It was reaching down to the plums on the ends of the branches and having a feed. I was delighted; it would be the first squirrel we have seen here in Waterford. As I looked closer, however, I noticed that it had no bushy tail, and then realised that I was looking at a good-sized rat! I ran out; it leapt off the tree, landing with a thump in the grass, and scurried away into the hedge. We have watched carefully since then, and have not seen it again, but it has made us think twice about our organic plums.

There is a perfume in the evening air from the musk rose that is in bloom at the side of the cottage. This rose has been giving olfactory pleasure for many decades: it is grown from a cutting I took from a bush that was growing against the front wall of the nearby Hayes farmhouse after it had been abandoned. The same bush can be seen in photographs taken by my father of the Hayes family in the 1930s.

Kilcop, 13 July

Although it is hard graft at times, I enjoy working in the open air, and even after the annual clearing and cutting back of the jungle advance has been completed, I can always find something interesting and useful to do outdoors. If the weather is good, I spend much of my time in Kilcop pottering about 'on the land'. Today I needed to pot some plants into bigger tubs, and as I was filling some tubs with clay I was charmed by a dark-spotted, chestnut-coloured green fritillary landing beside me, a rare butterfly to me. It had a piece missing from one wing, and must have been blown well off course by the strong winds we've been having over the last few days, because its normal habitat is sand dunes, where its caterpillars feed on violets. The nearest sand dunes to us are at Tramore, nine kilometres away. This butterfly's cousin, the silver-washed fritillary, is a more common visitor, and is another insect beauty with tawny orange wings speckled with black. It's no wonder this particular butterfly likes it here in Kilcop; it feeds on brambles and thistles.

Another job I've been working at is completing my 'around the field' sand walk. I was cutting through the undergrowth down at Gobbo's Garden when I disturbed a magpie moth, a pretty insect with white wings decorated with a black and orange design. Its Latin name, *Abraxas grossulariata*, sounds far too complicated for such a pretty little creature. No wonder it was hanging about in Gobbo's Garden: the larvae feed on blackthorn, privet and hawthorn, of which there is no shortage in that spot.

There has been a year-on-year reduction of moths here in Kilcop; whereas in the 1980s, early every summer morning, we would frequently count ten or twelve different species around the outside light and on the bathroom window. Each one would be identified in our insect recognition book, with the date we saw it noted next to the illustration. Some of them were exceptionally beautiful, such as the 'garden tiger', the red underwing, the pine hawkmoth, which looked like a fallen leaf, and the very exotic, startling pink elephant hawkmoth. I regret that I have seen none of these in recent years.

Bats are also decreasing in numbers, which concerns me particularly. Are they, like the moths, on their way to becoming partially extinct in the Kilcop area? And are more fundamental extinctions on the way? The corn bunting was a common countryside bird in County Waterford, but the great changes in farming practices, particularly the loss of the kind of mixed farming that was carried out on the farm of which our field was a part, have led to its extinction. It pains me to think that, in a small way, the development of our cottage has assisted in at least one extinction. It is, however, the disappearance of a vast number of unknown tiny insect species, together with bees, beetles, butterflies, moths and flies, which will cause problems in the future.

British statistics show that ten species of beetle, nine of bees, wasps and ants, and eighteen of moths and butterflies have become extinct since the 1990s. A recent German study produced startling results: it involved capturing insects in special tents, and the weight of the insects caught has fallen by 76 per cent in twenty-seven years.

The nutrients that moths rely on are mainly consumed at their larval stage, so in adulthood they feed mainly on liquids, obtained from flowers in the form of nectar and from trees in the form of sap. In the neighbourhood of our cottage, many of the fields and hedges have been ecologically transformed over the last four decades. There are houses and outbuildings, lawns, decks and tarmac now in place of wildflower-rich meadows, and the original thick, mixed-species hedges have been bulldozed out and replaced by concrete walls and timber fences. In some cases, I have seen trees cut down simply because they are a nuisance and cover the tarmac in autumn with

wet leaves. In these circumstances there is little left
for moths; the pollination work they did no longer
takes place, and the creatures that rely on them for
their food, such as other insects, frogs, shrews,
hedgehogs, bats and birds, will also suffer, with
further downstream effects.

Years ago, when the bats were plentiful and the
children were young, I was jolted awake at half-past
three one morning by what I thought were the panic-
stricken cries of Donal, our youngest, in the throes
of a nightmare. I leapt out of bed to get to him before
he woke the others, but realised it was my daughter
Fiona's voice, not Donal's, shouting 'A bird! A bird!'
In the bunkroom where the children slept I found a
bat fluttering around the room in a figure-of-eight
pattern.

Suddenly it 'landed' on the wall near the ceiling,
upside down, barely holding onto the sand/cement
finish with its tiny claws, its wings folded up tight.
It had a strange shape – Donal said it looked just
like a bit of crumpled brown paper on the wall. The
creature was looking around, from side to side, its
eyes bright and tiny ears erect, its mouth pouting in
a 'kiss-kiss' shape. I got the children up and into the
other room, while I considered what I was going to do
with it.

I opened the front door, hoping the bat would
follow the cool air and escape. Then I shone my torch
at it and it launched itself, upside down, into flight
again. I ducked as it whirred over me, back and forth,
before taking up the same perch again. Again and
again it launched itself, looking for an escape route,
but failed. Teresa suggested getting a sweeping brush

and a large supermarket bag and tipping him carefully into the bag. An eminently sensible idea, I thought, and it worked out perfectly. During one of its perching periods I easily tipped the bat into the bag with the brush. It was squeaking and yelping, almost like a miniature dog barking. I quickly closed the bag and we all cheered!

We took the bag outside, and when the children were ready and watching I gently tipped the animal out onto the path. It tumbled about a little, and when I reached out and stroked its back, it made great attempts to bite me with its tiny teeth! It was clear that the bat couldn't take off from the ground, so I nudged it onto a flat piece of wood and gently raised it off the path. Swiftly and deftly, the bat swung itself to hang upside down off the edge of the piece of wood and launched into the night!

Our bunkroom bat had a wingspan of about 20cm, so it was probably pipistrelle. It had dark-brown fur with a suede-like texture, its eyes were big and black, its face almost a concave, with an ingrown nose. What a sight and what a night!

Kilcop, 15 July
I had a glorious, full-tide swim in Woodstown at five o'clock yesterday afternoon: on good sunny days the tide comes in over hot sands and the water can be as warm as the Mediterranean. As often happens, mullet came in with the rising tide and were jumping in silver flashes clean out of the water around me. I haven't experienced this at any other Irish beach; it's idyllic.

I should know almost every single grain of sand on Woodstown beach by this stage. Our father would take us there for a swim on a summer's evening, when he finished work. My mother would pack a picnic tea, and minutes after arriving on the fine, white, seashell-covered sands, we'd be in the water. Dad wasn't a great swimmer – breaststroke and sidestroke were his pace – but he loved floating, toes in the air, coasting over swells and waves. These vivid golden memories are still strong – one can almost feel that warm evening sun and hear the quiet rustle of the tiny waves on the shelly shore. If the tide was still rising, we children would make a sand boat at the water's edge, prow to the sea, decorated with many cockle and razor shells, and we jump up and down with excitement as the incoming waves steadily eroded the boat around us and came flooding in.

Kilcop, 16 July
We have a pair of grey-backed crows nesting in one of the trees in the front hedge, and since there is lots of activity there, they must be rearing a second or third brood. When we first built the cottage, a grey-backed used to come early every morning and wake us. It gave us a bit of a fright, because the first we knew of its visit was an insistent knocking on the kitchen window, as if someone needed us urgently. I jumped out of our pull-out bed and ran to the window, but when I pulled the curtain there was no one there. It was a ghostly kind of mystery that we wondered about, until the following morning when the same thing happened. Fortuitously, there was a gap between the curtains, and before I pulled them, the mystery was solved when I glimpsed, through the gap, a large crow perched on the window sill, pecking away at the

glazing putty, which was still fresh. Apparently, birds are attracted to the linseed oil in the putty. We had to put wire mesh over the window to try to dissuade it, but the bird continued to come at 6 a.m. every morning to strut up and down the window sill, loudly cawing, before trying to get its beak through the wire. He sometimes brought items with him, maybe to offer as gifts to his reflection in the glass; we found some small coins and two mussel shells on different occasions. It also left what my mother would politely have termed his 'calling card', and, more than once, coughed up a 'pellet' of plastic bag remains and grit on the sill.

When we really tired of these early alarm calls, we arranged wire along the sill to make it a less hospitable perch, and we weren't bothered again; we did, however, have to re-putty the window, and wondered afterwards why he didn't seem to be interested in the other windows. I remember a time when grey-backed crows, targeted by gamekeepers and farmers for their predatory habits, were rare, but they are everywhere today, including suburban Dublin.

Kilcop, 17 July
I am constantly reinforcing the hedges around our field, particularly the hedge to the laneway. Unchoppable logs from the bigger trees that I have cut down go into the hedge, and also barrowloads of cuttings, trimmings, grass, and, the other day, a heavy barrowload from the gateway, which annually has to be cleared of mud brought down the road after torrential rain. At the back of the airing barns I have erected for stacking and drying timber logs, the hedge

has also received a variety of offerings, from broken glassware and delph to old floor tiles and ashes from the fire. It's a formidable hedge anyway, with an old retaining wall at its centre, because the ground level in our field is nearly a metre higher than that of the surface of the lane outside. In the early days, when the foliage was thinner, I strung a sheepwire fence along it, but the fence has long ago disappeared in the growth and foliage that now creates a solid screen.

When we bought Kilcop, there were three old elms in this hedge. They were English elms, most of which, in Ireland and elsewhere, contracted Dutch elm disease, which killed them, so they had to be felled. Elm trees, however, have extensive root systems close to the ground, and since those elms were felled we have had a widespread occurrence of suckers – small elm trees – popping up along the line of the hedge. Some of them are substantial and grow to about six metres high, but when they get to about fifteen years old, they tend to die. I'm told that this is because the elm disease is spread by a beetle which is attracted to elm flowers, so until the tree is mature enough to produce a flower, it is safe, but you will rarely see a mature elm. Before our suckers get to that stage, I cut them down; they tend to have a diameter of about 175mm, and they make for a good-sized log and reasonably good firing. I leave the stumps standing a metre high in the hedge, like fence posts, and before long they start to sprout again.

Kilcop, 20 July
We were visited today in Kilcop by a magnificent dragonfly. I was sitting out drinking my morning

tea when I thought I heard a little bird fluttering in the foliage behind me. Next minute, what I thought first was a small bird coasted past me and around the corner of the house. Following it, I saw it was a dragonfly, and when it landed on a rhododendron leaf, I was able to get a good look at it. It was a huge and magnificent creature, with wings like smoked glass, spanning about a hundred metres. Its body was brilliantly coloured with turquoise and red spots and its eyes were huge, almost 6mm in diameter.

Later I caught sight of a brief but fascinating scene: a wood pigeon, flying as fast as possible in level flight, shot by over the west hedge, followed closely and swiftly by a sparrowhawk, which in turn was being mobbed and darted at by three little swallows. All five of them disappeared behind the trees at the bottom of the field, and I never did learn the result of their exertions.

Kilcop, 22 July
Last night we had the first rain in three weeks. Teresa and I watched, listened to and smelled the downpour while sitting in the shelter of the porch, as if we were welcoming a monsoon in the Far East. Today dawned, so dramatically unlike the previous weeks, dull and misty: it's like another country. It didn't last long, however; by noon the sun was out burning off the last of the mists. There was a low tide in the afternoon and we went swimming at a nearby beach called The Saleens. The beach there lines the inlet through which the Atlantic twice daily inundates the Back Strand of Tramore, and there is a magical period at low tide when the last of the Back Strand

water drains into the sea through some deep sandy pools. Swimming in these crystal-clear pools is most refreshing, and if one has a snorkel, there are baby squid and a variety of fish to be seen. Upstream, little egrets stalk the shallows with a family of herons. The sandbanks of the Back Strand produce lots of cockles: I have to admit that I have never, yet, harvested or eaten this shellfish, which used to be popular when I was a boy.

Kilcop, 23 July

Today as I work in the 'garden' of Kilcop in the heat of a summer's day, I am reminded that up to fifty years ago, farm workers laboured in this field, ploughing, sowing and bringing in the harvest. I have a photograph of the harvest in progress in this very field, with Tom Hayes supervising. It shows waistcoated labourers in their shirtsleeves throwing stooks of hay up onto the harvester with pitchforks, where two other men feed the stooks into the maw of the machine. One man wears a battered hat, while the others wear caps, with the peaks to the back. Tom oversees a man at ground level who is filling jute sacks with the grain. The harvester is timber-built and iron-wheeled, and is driven by way of a long leather drive belt from a chugging, ancient and battered Ferguson tractor.

I am very conscious that these men were labouring for their living, which was hard won over fifty years ago, while the work I do in Kilcop today is for the pleasure of it. Fifty years ago, the field, through a wise policy of crop rotation (before the word 'sustainability' had been invented) had produced potatoes, wheat, oats, mangels and barley, and in between times had provided sweet herbage for grazing cows.

I have good childhood memories of the Hayes family and the farm that was here in the 1950s, and of harvest time. The strongest memories are olfactory, and one is of the smell of sweat mingled with boiled spuds that filled the Hayes farmhouse when these lean but muscular men, all sadly long gone, sat at a trestle table laden down with great steaming tureens of potatoes, plates with slabs of ham, bowls of country butter, and mugs of tea, and tucked lustily into their lunch. They needed it; the couple of times that I cut and stacked hay in our field in the early days I found it back-breaking work. In those days when there were haystacks in the haggard, we children used to climb up onto them and lie down in the sun. The wonderful smell, the warmth and smooth quality of the hay is still a strong memory, as is the fearful thrill of sliding down off the stacks, which must have been seven feet, to the ground.

Well into the twentieth century, the Hayes farm was a 'mixed' farm, in the full meaning of the term. They had cattle to provide milk, cream and butter, hens for eggs, and they also kept pigs. They had a fine big horse for carting and ploughing, and they would have had some fields under wheat or barley. In those days our acre field, in a good year, would have produced one and a half tons of wheat. The by-product of wheaten straw was built into the haystacks we used to slide down and used for animal bedding. The meadow fields were fertilised with farmyard manure from the cattle, pigs, hens and the horse. The diet of the cattle that grazed these meadows would have been augmented with chopped mangels, oats, and hay, and possibly some linseed cake, the only foodstuff that was actually bought in.

Potatoes and a range of vegetables were grown in a field just across the road from the farmhouse. Tom's mother, Mary Hayes, kept beehives at the back of the house for the production of honey. Some of the milk was taken in churns by cart to the creamery, and the rest made into butter using a wooden churn of a design that dates back centuries, of oak staves bound together with iron straps. I well remember, as a child, not liking this 'country butter', because it was so salty. Eggs and cream were taken to town by Mary Hayes in her pony and trap, and sold.

It was my childhood memories of the Hayes farm, and reading of Michael and Ethna Viney and their search for self-sufficiency in Mayo, that led us to decide to buy a little land in familiar, rural Waterford. Tom Hayes agreed to sell us an acre field in Kilcop, and, borrowing most of the money, we did the deal, and became rural landowners. In the field we built a tiny cottage, which we called 'The Little House on the Prairie', consisting of a kitchen and living area, a bunk room for the children, and a bathroom. Teresa and I slept in the living area on a pull-out bed. We were also admirers of John Seymour and his inspiring book, *Self-Sufficiency*, and enjoyed the knowledge that, if everything went downhill, we could almost grow sufficient food on the acre to feed our family. If we got a suitable and easily handled inshore boat, we could supplement our diet with fish, and cockles, mussels and razor fish could be harvested from Woodstown beach. It was an enjoyable, but probably very naive daydream!

It was not something we thought about at the time, but in building a cottage on farming land we were contributing to ribbon development, a particularly Irish disease that is destructive of farmland, and is socially, economically and environmentally unsustainable. Poor rural and urban planning has led to our built environment flooding out of the cities and eating up the countryside. The result of not learning from other countries and planning for village-centred rural development has led to our Disneyland bungalow countryside, each house served by an unmonitored septic tank, many of which are polluting the ground around them. Village or hamlet gatherings of dwellings would produce sustainable communities, economically centralising amenities and services such as sewerage, garbage collection, electricity provision, a postal service, and telecommunications. Instead, overextended supply lines are needed to deliver essential services, and as the people who live in these scattered dwellings grow old and isolated, they face problems of loneliness, vulnerability and fear. I am sure that the current problem of the sustainability of rural post offices and small shops would not be so acute if village cluster development had been encouraged.

In England 97 per cent of traditional meadows have disappeared since the 1940s, a fact revealed by Luftwaffe aerial reconnaissance photographs taken during the war. Here in Ireland we cannot be far off this percentage; almost all our grassland is now intensively farmed with the abundant application of herbicides and fertilizers, so there are few traditional meadows left.

I can remember Tom Hayes telling me of pine

martens in the trees around his house, and corncrakes in the fields. While pine martens are coming back in some parts of the west of Ireland, meadow-loving corncrakes have practically disappeared, and only those in their later years have memories of hearing them in the Irish countryside. They are only to be found today in a few western counties, or on Tory Island, off County Donegal, where I first heard them. During my time there, morning, evening and even late at night, corncrakes could be heard.

One evening, taking a stroll westwards from the village on the island, I decided to see if I could catch a glimpse of one. Because there are no hedges on Tory, there was little cover for wildlife other than occasional thick and tall patches of nettles. I walked across a field in the direction of the call that seemed nearest. The farther I walked, however, the farther away it seemed, and I had almost given up when suddenly a corncrake emerged from a clump of nettles a couple of metres in front of me. A smooth, speckled and very elegant, pipette-shaped bird, it was beautifully lit up by the low evening sun. It moved along, gently ducking and bowing as it went, not appearing to take a lot of notice of me, but sidling away nevertheless. I stood enthralled as it eventually disappeared into some long grass. It was a delightful experience. In my euphoria I had forgotten to use my camera.

Kilcop, 26 July
Today, we took the car ferry across the river from Passage East in Munster to Ballyhack in Leinster, and drove to Hook Lighthouse, the eastern portal of Waterford Harbour. There we sat on great dark

grey shelving slabs of carboniferous limestone that step down from the ancient lighthouse to meet the Atlantic, looking out to the edge of the world to the south, and across to the red sandstone cliffs of County Waterford to the east. Our seat was made up of the fossilised shells and hard parts of a myriad of sea creatures that had lived and died over many thousands of years, more than 325 million years ago, 300 million years before the world was ruled by dinosaurs. In the midst of a forest of crinoids, palm-tree-like marine animals related to starfish, these sea creatures thrived in a shallow tropical sea located, at that time, somewhere in what is today the south-west Atlantic. Imagining the world as it was then, many millions of years before even the dinosaurs arrived, puts the brief existence of our human kind into a startling perspective.

I have been sitting in the pitch dark looking at the night sky and listening to that hiss of silence, a very definite and audible hiss. Or maybe it's just my ears singing with relief to be resting in a quiet place. Nowadays noise is a permanent part of our life in cities, never ceasing, not always loud or necessarily unpleasant, but always present. Now and again a car passes on the nearby road, intruding on the aural scene, and at regular intervals a crop protector punctuates the silence with a thudding loudness, but in between, there's a silence that hisses.

In the space of fifteen minutes, three space satellites moved brightly across the sky, their brightness reducing as they 'descended' towards

the horizon. I well remember my father calling
me out into the garden in October 1957 to see the
Russian satellite Sputnik. It was a moment of great
excitement. Today such miracles of modern science
are commonplace in the sky at night, if you only look
out for them. The statistics are thought-provoking:
the United Nations Office for Outer Space Affairs
report that since Sputnik I, 8,377 objects have been
launched into space, and currently nearly 5,000 are
in orbit.

By II.45 p.m. a great cloud of stars was visible
across the sky, which is bisected by the dense Milky
Way. Stars that were noted on their own earlier
in the evening can now, in the dark, be seen to
be surrounded by clusters of seemingly close
companions, and every now and then a dart of light
seen from the corner of the eye betrayed a shooting
star. On only a couple of occasions did I see one
directly – it is such an exhilarating sight.

When the children were much younger, we used
to take out the mattresses from the bunk beds and
lay them on the ground, so that we all could watch
the heavens without getting a crick in our necks. It
reminded me of W.H. Auden's 'A Summer Night':

> Out on the lawn I lie in bed,
> Vega conspicuous overhead
>   In the windless nights of June,
> As congregated leaves complete
> Their day's activity; my feet
>   Point to the rising moon.

Kilcop, 29 July

A year or two after we divided our original acre field in two, the half-acre to the east of the cottage began to become a bother. The meadow grass grew well on it, but I would have needed a tractor to cut it every year, and although it produced excellent grass, I couldn't find anyone interested in mowing it. For one year I provided it to a neighbour for grazing a small herd of heifers. While there was no monetary payment, I did, of course, benefit in that these animals manured the land. There may not seem to be a more prosaic thing than manure, but the humble cowpat is another little-understood example of the magic of nature. Sitting on the surface of the ground, it is the gathering place for a myriad of insects, as many as 200 different species, many of them laying their eggs in it and recycling the dung. The insects, a host of bacteria and the broken-down dung in the cowpat enrich the soil and provide food for many other insects in a powerful, unseen and unending cycle of nature.

Unfortunately, in this case, after the animals had left, the enriched soil produced great grass, but with no one to harvest it; it fell over, rotted and became rank. I was delighted to agree when a local man, Peter, asked me if he could graze a couple of his donkeys in the field. Their existence added greatly to our country experience. The donkeys used to give our children a loud greeting of 'hee-haws' when we arrived from Dublin, and during the time we spent in Kilcop they got used to coming over to the dividing fence to get sheaves of long fresh grass that the children would collect for them.

Eventually the female donkey became pregnant, and we watched her as the weeks went by, not thinking that we would be there when she gave birth. One morning, however, when I got up early and looked out the bedroom window, the first thing I saw was the female donkey standing quietly near the fence, with two little legs protruding from her backside. I hurried to get the children out of bed; they had their American cousins staying at the time, so there was a good audience for the birth.

It took about fifteen minutes in all, as the mother crouched down and then lay down, and began to heave and roll about a little. The donkey baby emerged bit by bit, wrapped in what looked like a plastic bag, which the American cousins immediately called its 'survival suit'. The mother didn't seem distressed at any time, and she lay there languorously until the umbilical cord followed the baby out. When the foal began stretching the 'plastic bag' this way and that, trying to remove it from its head, the mother got to her knees and began to lick it, quickly removing the membrane. By then the foal was on its knees as well.

The children were amazed by the whole event, and by the fact that the baby donkey got to its feet within twenty minutes of being born, and stood beside the mother, legs akimbo.

A few years later, however, Peter sold his donkeys, and our half-acre was left fallow again. I hated to see the grass going rank in it, and but for one stand of purple loosestrife in the middle of the field, most of the wildflowers had disappeared. Eventually, we decided to sell it. Third-level education is expensive, perhaps our greatest expenditure after our mortgage, and we needed the money. We reluctantly sold the land for a good price, and, after paying capital gains tax, ended up with a sufficient sum to cover the educational fees for a few years. I planted a hawthorn hedge and a linear shrubbery along our new eastern boundary. It took some years to come to maturity, but today we are hedged all round.

By the end of July I had sawn almost all the timber that had been harvested in previous months, and in particular I enjoyed sawing a big thick ash trunk, 225mm in diameter, revealing about eighteen years of growth. I have now filled the larger of my airing barns with five rows of logs, and I gaze at them with pleasure and a little sense of achievement every time I pass it. It should provide at least three years' timber supply for my two solid fuel stoves in Glendoher, and I still have more of the smaller branches to saw. The timber harvested amounts to only about 10 per cent of the trees in Kilcop, and I'm told our remaining trees provide a sufficient carbon sink to more than offset the result of burning my own fuel.

We have come to the end of our long summer sojourn in Kilcop, and while there are some regrets, we are looking forward to returning to Glendoher.

Glendoher, 31 July

When we arrive back in Glendoher after a long absence, one of the first things we do is investigate the back garden, to see which plants have come on and which have died, usually because of lack of water. Today we found that the busy birdsong of May and June was absent, probably because many of our avian delights are moulting, and during this period, with their ability to fly slightly hampered, they tend to hide away in the undergrowth.

Moulting is an annual affair: many birds' feathers are delicate, and they wear out or can be damaged. Feathers, like our fingernails, are made from keratin, and if damaged, they do not regrow or heal, and have to be replaced. During moulting, new replacement feathers push out the old ones: it is a gradual process, occurring in sequence across the bird's body so that there are no bald patches. Small birds take as many as five weeks to complete the process, and during that time they stay out of sight. In the garden I was delighted to find, floating on the pond, a brown-barred cream feather that I feel must have been shed by our local sparrowhawk. Although we rarely find the moulted feathers of small birds, those that larger birds have left behind are easily collected during this period; they can make a beautiful display in a vase.

August

No wind, no bird. The river flames like brass.
On either side, smitten as with a spell
Of silence, brood the fields. In the deep grass,
Edging the dusty roads, lie as they fell
Handfuls of shriveled leaves from tree and bush.

– Lizette Woodworth Reese, 'August'

kestrel

Glendoher, 4 August
Today we awoke to find flocks of magpies mercilessly
worrying and mobbing the sparrowhawk family that
nest in the Spinney. Up to a dozen magpies at a time
were constantly diving on, perching next to and
chasing the birds in flight, with the hawks fighting
back, producing marvellous dogfights. I'm surprised
that the hawks are still nesting in the Spinney,
because every year they have to put up with the same
harassment. But they continue to nest there, in spite
of annual efforts to dislodge them. Today I got some
good photographs of the aerial battles; the strong
sunlight provided good well-lit shots, including one
or two of the hawks banking in formation, exposing
their beautiful speckled undersides.

Birdwatch Ireland claims that sparrowhawks are
widespread and the most common bird of prey in
Ireland, but although I have regular sightings of the

birds, they are mainly my local ones: I would have thought that the smaller kestrel, frequently seen hovering in the sky, is far more common. Perhaps the sparrowhawk's shy and secretive nature is the reason it is not spotted more often.

We had a swarm of ants in the garden today. It usually happens when the breeze is in the right direction and the warmth of the sun creates suitable thermals to allow the insects to take easily to the air. This phenomenon is called the mating swarm or the nuptial flight, and occurs when young queens set out to establish new nests, together with male ants, with whom they will mate on the wing. Garden ants have their extensive nests out of sight under patios or paving slabs, and each year, at some signal of nature, many thousands of winged ants pour out of the nests and take to the air. Today I was working in the garden when it happened. One minute all was normal, and the next the pavings and the grass were alive with the ants, the silver slivers of their wings gleaming in the sun like some animated liquid. At every moment dozens of ants were taking flight, while some of them wandered around for a while before attempting to get into the air. A few just couldn't get the hang of it, and stumbled about, trying to get their wings to work. Many wingless ants, the workers, had also turned out, running to and fro, to see the queens and males off. Above the field we noted passing gulls darting, circling and diving, almost like swallows or bats, to feed on the ants on the wing.

When the queen has mated, she drops to the ground, chews off her wings, and establishes a new ant colony. The sperm she has stored will last her for a lifetime, which can amount to many years, during which she will continue to produce thousands of fertilised eggs.

The swarming is amazing to behold. My sister Olivia, who is on holidays with us from Texas and is no stranger to exotic nature, was astonished by it.

Ticknock, 7 August
I had a wonderful walk today, familiarising myself again with our local gorse- and heather-covered Ticknock. Showers were threatening, and the forecast was bad, but I went anyway, braving the rain in my shirtsleeves, and I was glad I did. The heather is beginning to bloom, and the perfumes were strong, in spite of a light breeze. There may be a number of varieties of heather on this hill, but there are only two that I can identify: ling heather and bell heather. Ling, with small, purple flowers tight to the stalk, is the dominant plant in the acid soils of the Dublin Mountains, and, like most common plants, it had many uses in former times, from a flavouring for beer to its use in making long-lasting brooms for sweeping. Bell heather has larger, bell-shaped flowers that are more pink than purple.

All the autumn wildflowers were out, and gorse and heather proclaimed the Wexford colours all over the hill. The icing-like blossom of the silverweed and all the mauves and purples of the various thistles, eyebright, that tiny white flower with the yellow eye, and the constant celandine decorated the verges of the forestry road. The fraughans were in full fruit in the old herb-clothed wall running along the Wicklow Way, and I purpled my hands harvesting and eating an abundance of the berries, which are rich in antioxidants. This delicious wild fruit, much associated with the festival of Lúnasa, has many names in Ireland, including whortleberry in my home county of Waterford and mossberry in Donegal. During Lúnasa in the old days, boys made bracelets of fraughans and vied with each other to get the prettiest girl to accept and wear theirs. In County Longford wine was made with the berries, and young lovers would drink it to hasten their wedding day.

The mountain skies were majestic, and although I could see the curtains of a few showers a long way off to the south, the visibility was good: the storied and sacred hill of Crohaun, where I am sure celebrations took place at Lúnasa, was in sight to the west, rising from the flatness of the Bog of Allen, and the Mourne Mountains loomed in the north. On the eastern horizon, the blue-grey rounded shapes of Holyhead Mountain and Snowdonia rose above the Irish Sea horizon.

As I was coming down towards the forestry, I experienced an unusual sight. At a particular time of a particular day in late summer, conifers make use of a light breeze to puff out and broadcast yellow clouds of pollen; this is how conifers cross-pollinate, rather than with the help of birds or insects. It is a surreal and even mystical thing to see. At the time of pollination, a tree's seed cones are quite small, but when pollination takes place, they grow quickly and produce seeds. I'm told that this particular method of cross-pollination goes back to a primordial time when primitive tree ferns and mosses dominated the earth's plant life.

Before my walk was finished, a great dark layer of cloud moved up north-eastwards out of Kildare, hydroplaning on a curtain of light grey rain. As I reached the car and drove down towards the main road, I could see that it was an extensive front, still sliding northwards with no trailing edge in sight: it had progressed across the north city and suburbs, and it looked as if it might sideswipe the southern suburbs. When I got home, we had just time to take in the clothes off the line, before a fifteen-minute downpour swept through.

Ticknock, 11 August

I usually come back from holidays in Waterford a few pounds heavier than when I went, probably because of lack of regular climbing exercise and, of course, too much eating and drinking. That's the reason why I found myself up Ticknock again this morning in hazy weather with black clouds to the south-west moving in. Two sparrowhawks were circling and playing with each other just above the gun butts. As I came to the junction where the road heads right for the Wicklow Way, another large bird, light brown in colour, flew above me, very near, and settled in a conifer. It moved off as I approached, but lazily, as if unconcerned about my presence. A little farther on, I saw it rise out of a large clump of thistles, and it hung suspended on the breeze. When the other two birds, seen earlier, turned up, the third bird joined them and they began jinking and diving at each other. I suspect the third bird was the mother.

Purple thistles were blooming beside the road now and attracting oceans of butterflies, particularly painted ladies, but in one stand I also saw peacocks, red admirals, small tortoiseshells and small cabbage butterflies. The painted lady is in the news this week, and the seven I counted here must have been a few of the many thousands that have been reported as being spotted crossing into Ireland over the Wexford coast. On the radio I heard the presenter of a morning show using the unfortunate term 'a plague of painted ladies' when he was referring to the phenomenon. This is a remarkable butterfly, spreading northwards in huge migrations from the deserts of North Africa annually to reach Europe, sometimes arriving in Ireland in great swarms, as it has in the past week. Strangely, because the adult does not live longer than a few weeks, it takes more than one generation to complete the migration to Ireland: along the way, they mate and reproduce before dying. The generation that arrives here feeds on thistles, mates, reproduces, and sets off back towards Africa as soon as the weather turns cold again.

Gorse flowers were spreading their pleasant fragrance, a fragrance that hints so much to me of coconut, although some say it smells of oranges. This well-known shrub is more commonly known in the northern part of Ireland as whin, and in the southern part as furze, which I believe is a Scandinavian name. In County Waterford it was called gorse, and I have always used that name for it. For such an unforgiving, threatening, prickly shrub, often gnarled and scrawny, the gorse bush produces an exquisite flower. Look at it close up and feel it; it has a silky and most delicate blossom in purest yellow. Its brilliant yellow flowers set alight wild and undeveloped areas of countryside, and it is often the first strong colour of spring in

Ireland, holding out until the wildflowers get going. Gorse, however, often flowers a number of times a year, notably even in January, giving 'Tokens to the wintry earth that beauty liveth still'. Another saying about the shrub is 'When gorse is out of season, kissing's out of favour'. Ireland seems to have a climate that perfectly suits the shrub, although I have seen it growing happily in Spain and Italy. It is said that when Carl Linneaus, the eighteenth-century Swedish explorer and naturalist, first saw gorse in flower on Wimbledon Common, he fell to his knees to thank Heaven for such a glorious sight; this sounds a bit over the top, but he did carefully cultivate a gorse plant in his greenhouse at Uppsala in Sweden. It is so common and vigorous in Ireland, and grows so well on poor land, that great efforts have been made over the centuries to find a use for it as a crop, and it was formerly important to the rural economy of large areas of Ireland. In the Civil Survey of 1654–6, land where it grew is named specifically as 'furzy' or 'furzy pasture' and classified as 'profitable'. Traditionally, when in young shoot form, it was a very nutritious food for animals, and, crushed in a mill, it was used as a bonding material in mud walls. The ashes of burnt gorse are still used today as a garden plant dressing.

I really enjoy it when, on hot, dry summer days, gorse legumes burst, just like broom, with a cracking noise, broadcasting the seeds some distance away:

> Love you not, then, to list and hear,
> The crackling of the gorse-flowers near,
> Pouring an orange-scented tide
> Of fragrance o'er the desert wide …
>
> – Alfred William Howitt, 'A Summer Noon'

Kilcop, 17 August

We're back again in Kilcop catching the tail end of
the summer. A few days ago, Teresa and I picked six
pounds of blackberries from the hedges on a nearby
lane. It was a beautiful sunny afternoon, the best kind
for picking, and the berries were in good shape. It's
an interesting and very satisfying country occupation
which we both enjoy, and both our childhoods are
laced with memories of warm early autumn days spent
blackberry-picking. My maternal grandfather was a
most enthusiastic picker, and used to hang a Kellogg's
Cornflakes box by string around his neck so that he
could use both hands for the work. The freshness of
the open air, the natural free food, the close brushes
with rude and basic nature such as nettles, brambles,
wasps, stink bugs and all kinds of other insects, and
the fact that we were all doing it together made it a
special activity. We all, including my grandfather,
used to end the day with 'purple-stained mouth'.

There is another side to the blackberry bush,
however. Before all the trees and shrubs were planted
in Kilcop and began to thrive, the brambles of the
hedges had unrestricted access to the field. The earth
in some areas had been disturbed during building
work, digging for drains, the septic tank and our well,
and it was these places that seemed to be singled out
by the thorny shrub, arching its tendrils over and
over again into a matrix of impenetrable thorns.
One summer I declared Bramble War, and set out
with slash hook and secateurs to push back the unruly
invader. Although a prickly war, with blood spilled,
it was a satisfying task, and my piercings reminded
me of the words in an old Irish tale of the king of *Dál
nAraidi* and his description of bramble thorns:

O briar, little arched one,
Thou grantest no fair terms,
Thou ceasest not to tear me,
Till thou hast thy fill of blood.

It was a few weeks before I had all the brambles cut to the root and burned. Then the roots themselves had to be dug out of the ground to prevent new growth sprouting the following year. I have enjoyed a lifetime of eating the fruit of the bramble in jam and tarts, but during Bramble Wars I gained a great respect for the plant. Its Latin name, *Rubus fruticosus*, does not hint at its wicked thorns or its remarkable invasive powers, but allude instead to its fruit, which has been regarded as a valuable food source since earliest times. Teresa remembers as a child traipsing 'out the country' with other children to pick buckets of blackberries, which were brought back into town to a pub where they were sold based on weight. These berries were sold on again and made into dyes for colouring fabrics or for making ink. When looking into traditional uses of the plant, I was surprised to find that in former times it and its roots had many practical uses.

In County Mayo, when stripped of their thorns, tendrils were used to make baskets or creels, while all over the country similar stripped branches were split and dried to make excellent 'twine' or bindings for straw. Because of their anti-fungal, antiseptic and astringent properties, the leaves, roots and fruits were used in a wide range of medicaments for treating ailments such as kidney complaints, diarrhoea, swellings and burns.

Kilcop, 18 August

One the best things we planted in Kilcop is a
buddleia with a gold and purple, globular flowerhead.
I have noted that it attracts almost all the butterflies,
including the red admiral, the peacock, tortoiseshells,
painted ladies, cabbage whites and meadow browns,
and at night moths take the place of the butterflies to
graze on the blooms.

Today, in the sunshine, it was attracting hosts of
butterflies to the area in front of the cottage. Many
of them sit grazing on the blossoms, sharing them
with bees and bumblebees, while often the walls
of the cottage were decorated by red admirals and
peacocks that had satiated themselves on the buddleia,
and were sunning themselves, wings luxuriantly
opening and closing. When they were grazing on
the buddleia flower, they were so engrossed that
they took no notice of me coming quite near, and
close up I watched a red admiral perch on a blossom
as it prepared to drink. It is only up close like this
that one can appreciate the intricate detail of the
butterfly. This particular insect's antennae were like
tiny bulrushes, long and slender with black and white
bands, terminating in a white-tipped black top. You
have to be close to see the thick fur-like covering on
the insect's back, which splays out across its wings,
and to observe it uncurling its long proboscis and
sinking it into the tiny golden buddleia florets, one
after another. If a hoverfly or a bumblebee comes
near, a regal flap of the butterfly's brilliantly coloured
wings will dissuade it from landing. The peacock has
the same fur, although brownish, on its back, and of
course the two 'eyes' on its wings serve to warn off
other insects. I have also noticed a few night-flying

moths browsing in daytime on the buddleia, but last evening I was attracted by a vigorous shaking in the bush that was caused by more than a moth. It was still daylight, but all the butterflies were gone; instead, I saw that there were a lot of moths browsing and, in the middle of the bush, an opportunist robin was making a dart at one of them every few minutes. I cannot say I saw him succeed in the time I watched, but he certainly put a lot of effort into having a good supper.

I have stood at this bush at night and have felt gentle puffs of air from the wings of bats as they hoover up the night shift of moths that replace the butterflies of daytime. The eighteenth-century naturalist Gilbert White wrote in 1788 of a tame bat:

> I was much entertained last summer with a tame bat, which would take flies out of a person's hand. If you gave it any thing to eat, it brought its wings round before the mouth, hovering and hiding its head in the manner of birds of prey when they feed. The adroitness it shewed in shearing off the wings of the flies, which were always rejected, was worthy of observation, and pleased me much.

On one buddleia flower I saw a strange white spider, a ghost-like creature, standing still. I had to slip into the cottage to get my insect book to identify it, and when I came out again it was still there. It was a species of crab spider called *Misumena vatia*. They can be yellow or white, depending on the flower they inhabit, but in this case the creature was white and stood out against the gold and purple of the buddleia. Its abdomen had three indentations that looked a little like a face. The vatia is found in Europe and North America, where it is the best-known flower spider and can be quite large, with a length of 10mm, excluding legs. This one, however, is no more than 4mm, and I wouldn't have noticed it but for the fact I was right up close to the flowers.

I find it fascinating that just one shrub, when observed carefully and over time, can offer so much to someone interested in nature. This experience made clear to me how important it is to be constantly observant, and to allow no subtle flavour of the night or day, of the place or the season, of the colour or the light, to escape one's eye.

Sitting outside Kilcop at evening time there does not seem to be, at first glance, much going on. However, patience and careful observation will pick up the swallows that are twittering overhead, the clouds in the sky that are changing colour by the minute as the sun descends, and the flying insects of the night that are beginning to come out of their daytime hiding places and flex their wings. Then, a flickering form jerkily darts across my view; the first bat is out and warming up before going on a night-long hunt. The Gaelic name for a bat is *scaitáin leathair*, or 'leather wings', a very descriptive name. It never ceases to amaze me that so few people are aware that bats are common, even in suburban areas. Most people will say that they have never seen one, but they can be observed most summer evenings in many parts of suburbia, and above the back garden of my own Dublin home. I suppose people do not expect to see bats, and therefore they do not notice them. What they do see flitting across the evening sky is registered simply as a 'bird' or even a swallow, or perhaps a swift. Of course, if that flittering had caught their curiosity, and they had focussed on what was flittering, they would see that its shape was not that of a bird. And while a bird, born to fly, will coast through the air gracefully, frequently pausing its wingbeats to glide, the bat, while it can glide, as if it realises that it really doesn't belong in the air, rarely stops furiously pumping its wings. They are quite wonderful creatures, the only mammals capable of sustained flight, and in Ireland we have nine native species. Bats breed once a year and give birth, in early summer, to one baby. They are an important agent in controlling the numbers of certain insects and for the eight months of the year when they are not in hibernation, their aerial feasts include insects such as midges, moths, caddisflies, and daddy longlegs.

Kilcop, 20 August
This afternoon, I had been sawing even more wood for the winter fires, when, with the thud of a falling log, the soft drone of a passing bumblebee whispered to me to 'take a break'. I stopped my labours, and, finding a shaded seat, sat a while as the perspiration on my brow cooled in a gentle breeze. My sawing was the rhythmic, therapeutic, penultimate act in harvesting the last of my coppiced ash crop. The final act will be even more satisfying: stacking the logs neatly in serried rows in the airing barn, an open, roofed structure that I hammered together a few years ago from recycled building timbers and concrete tiles. The remains of this year's long-lived summer heat

and the wind will do the rest, drying out the prepared timber until it is fire-ready. The neatly stacked logs will make a most satisfying sight.

On my garden seat I settled into a still state, giving my eyes and ears the full run of my surroundings. There are few pastimes I find as pleasant and as soothing as just sitting, looking and listening in the garden. Each time I do so, the little natural world around me, although familiar, has something different going on. The greenness of high summer, fed by the unusually heavy spring rains and encouraged by the subsequent long days of sunshine, was everywhere dense and lush as the rising sap reached the end of its push for this year. I looked along the hedge, seeing how it was intertwined with the wreathy bindings and delicate blooms of perfumed woodbine, and over the grass of my rustic lawn, which was jewelled with globes of clover flower and stalks of golden hawksbit.

I would like to have more clover; it is a super meadow plant in that its flowers are a great attracter of bumblebees, the whole plant is enjoyed by livestock, and its roots are a natural nitrogen enricher of the soil. Charles Darwin wrote of how red clover and its prevalence is an example of how seemingly unrelated aspects of nature can in fact be intimately connected, something we need to be particularly aware of today. He pointed out that the clover can only be fertilised by the bumblebee, whose tongue is long enough to reach the flower's nectar. The continuation of clover growth therefore depends on the number of bumblebees there are in a district, but the bees' numbers can depend on the population of field mice in the same district, because field mice are partial to bumblebees' honey, and destroy their broods. The mice in turn are predated upon by cats, so the healthy continuation of clover growth in a district is largely governed by the number of cats in that district. Today, the number of cats will depend on the number of rural households in the district, and unfortunately most of these modern households will regard the red clover in their lawns as a weed.

The leaves of the ash trees were shimmering in the strong sunlight, and one could almost hear the fluttering of the garlands of butterflies that were paying final homage to the burgeoning buddleia blossoms, which are just beginning to wither. Somewhere in the oak tree at the end of the garden, where the yellowhammer, now long gone, used to sing his song of bread and butter, a chiffchaff had taken up station and was stating his case, tirelessly, over and over. A dragonfly zoomed past me, darting this way and that, hawking for insects and flies that were too small for me to see.

Kilcop, 22 August
Last August my son Colm set up the old telescope on the stoop to have a look at Jupiter. After a little while spent adjusting focus and direction, we succeeded in capturing the planet, as clear as a bell, with five of its moons. I have seen it before through a good pair of binoculars, but this was a special experience. Better still, back along the line Colm was able to find Saturn, tiny but clear, a brilliant bright ball surrounded by oval rings. Just using his phone, Colm calculated that Saturn was at that moment 1.3 billion kilometres away, which meant that the image

we had seen took about an hour to reach us. As we were taking down the telescope, a brighter than normal satellite passed over. Consulting his phone again, Colm was able to find out that this was the international space station. Brighter than ordinary satellites, it was still gleaming as it travelled towards the horizon.

On two occasions, some years ago now, when we were out at night absorbing the miracle of the sky, we were visited by ghost-like barn owls. While one usually hears the sound of a large bird passing close by, the owl is equipped with special feathers that allow swift but absolutely silent flight. On one occasion the bird flew right over our heads, and it was glimpsed only because we were looking up at the sky at the time and so the owl was reflected in what little light came from a nearby house. It was a strange experience, as if a golden-eyed ghost had passed by. One wonders how many sightings of these rare birds are missed because of their silence. On the second occasion, while the sighting lacked the silent drama of the first, we got a better look at the bird. We were sitting out watching the last of the light receding. It had been a very warm day and the outside light was attracting a swirling corona of flies and moths, which in turn attracted a few jerky attacks by bats. Into this milieu came, briefly, a gleaming barn owl, which circled a couple of times, its wings and extended 'finger' feathers brilliantly picked out by the light, before vanishing again.

While the barn owl is partial to moths, bats do not form a large part of its menu; maybe the bat's echo-location powers protect them from the owl's silent approach. The bird is more comfortable with shrews, mice, rats and beetles. It has an acute sense of hearing which allows it to find prey, such as a field mouse in the middle of a field, in pitch darkness. The barn owl does not make a nest; instead, it lays its eggs on what must be a smelly heap of disgorged pellets of animal fur, feathers and bone.

Only rarely have I heard a night-time call that must have been a barn owl. Rather than a gentle 'ooohh-oooh' one expects of an owl, it lets out a weird, strangled and prolonged shriek, a little similar to the call of a female fox.

Ticknock, 24 August

We are back in Dublin again after a great summer in the south-east. While I love the summer, I don't at all mind it giving way to autumn. I have been in countries where the weather is more or less the same every day, and no matter how warm and bright it was, I missed the constantly changing temperatures and skies of Ireland, and the very defined seasons we have. Autumn has its own special gifts, as, indeed, winter has; if I was able to change anything, it would be to shorten the winter darkness.

I took a walk today up Ticknock and followed a different route to what I normally take. I crossed an area of forest, long ago harvested, threading gingerly across a pale boneyard of bleached roots and branches of long-gone trunks. On the other side I climbed a track, surfaced with granite gravel, the remnants of an eroded mountain. My boots made a comfortable crunching sound just audible above the wailing of wind gusting through the nearby forest, which sometimes rose to a howl, the trees leaning impossibly back, in unison, to absorb the wind's punches. I had a feeling that the trees enjoy the wind, and how it makes them dance together.

Two ravens crossed the sky before me, coasting effortlessly into the wind, their wings angled into profiles like futuristic fighter planes, jet black against the watercolour clouds, clearly enjoying themselves, one of them flipping over and back, maybe trying to impress the other, perhaps a potential mate for next spring. One turned back and rode the wind sideways just over my head, gazing curiously down at me, before it blasted out of sight beyond the trees.

My knees were feeling the exertion, the result of a long and lazy summer. Many short stops helped, however, and allowed me to take in the wider world within my ken, the outlying Dublin foothills to the west, the ruins of the Hellfire Club on domed Montpelier, and the intricate chaotic matrix of the city spreading out to the north.

The heather was at its best, glorious Manhattan towers of spiky flowers, all shades between purple and pink. The wind was stronger out on the open moor, and it vigorously brushed the heath into a surging sea of swells and troughs. I could see that the fields to the west, carved with great labour from the bog centuries ago by the men of Kelly's Glen, were returning to nature, absorbed by spreading gorse, heather and bracken, their subdivisions delineated by a barely detectable palimpsest of ditches and banks.

As the ground levelled out, the path that I followed, the work of a modern *meitheal* (a working party) of mountainy men, gleamed onwards before me, stretching south into the hills. At last, with the city still at my back, the gentle curves of the next ridge of the mountains came into view. Their flanks were brushed purple by a mist of heather, highlighted by brilliant, biblical streaks of sunlight passing over the slopes, sculpting out ravines and the fretworks of ancient turf cuttings. The only scars to spoil the scene were the patches of Passchendaele-like harvested woods below the bog. Pausing briefly in the shelter of a fraughan hedge I have been visiting for years, I enjoyed nature's refreshment, a cupped palm-full of small but perfect, astringent purple beauties.

A little farther on I flushed a pair of grouse. Because red grouse are so well camouflaged and usually hide away in thick heather well clear of paths, they can be difficult birds to observe; the first one usually knows of their presence is when, as in this case, they burst out of the heather with an explosion of wingbeats, cackling their strange warning call, which almost sounds like 'go-back, go-back, go-back'.

Years ago, before I knew anything about grouse or had ever seen one, I was wandering alone in the mist through the heather on the flat top of Killakee Mountain, not far from Ticknock. I knew roughly where I was, and although I had no compass, I was hoping that I was heading in the right direction to get down into clear air. I got a bit of a start, to say the least, when I heard, nearby, what sounded to me at the time like the cackling of a typical fairy-tale hag, a hag that knew I was lost and was laughing at my foolishness. I was almost expecting her to materialise out of the mist, her crooked finger pointing at me as she shook her wrinkled head, but I heard no more. It was only later that I learned from a friend about the warning call of the grouse, which of course was what I had heard. Since then I have heard and seen them many times, and have even managed once to get up very close, unnoticed, as a pair fed on a heather meal. The mainstay of their mountain diet is ling heather, and they can find suitable parts of that plant to eat at all times of the year, from the seeds in autumn and winter to the young shoots in spring and summer. The red grouse is a beautiful bird, finely shaped and richly coloured, and it survives happily in the wild vegetation of high, bleak mountain moors. It is said that when it is snowing heavily, they have to keep treading with their feet to avoid being buried. They are strictly monogamous: the female lays between six and a dozen eggs, and although the male does not incubate the eggs, it seems that he makes himself generally useful in rearing and protecting the chicks.

The wind at my back helped me as I took on the last incline, breathing heavily but pushing myself, the muscles of my legs aching pleasurably. At the top I clambered up onto a granite tor, long carved by sun, wind and rain into the shape of a fossilised prehistoric monster. I sat to sip water, overlooking an expanse of Irish Sea stretching from Lambay Island down to beyond the Sugarloaf. The sky was heavy with fast-moving low clouds, grey with a tinge of purple. The sea was the colour of the sky, splashed in places with gleaming patches of pure silver where the sun penetrated the overcast. The eastern horizon was visible only in places, and in spite of the conditions, the grey, ghostly swell of Holyhead Mountain was vaguely in view. South of the Sugarloaf, dark curtains of rain were moving from the west into the Irish Sea. To the north, Dublin city sat quiet, the tide out, and the bay backed by crescents of wave-fringed sands sweeping around to the Hill of Howth. Beyond Howth, the islands of Ireland's Eye and Lambay were highlighted in sunbeams.

After a satisfying and restorative drink of water, I continued on along an ancient and much-eroded mearing bank. Swallows swiftly flitted back and forth across the heather, hoovering up an invisible meal – their low-level flight suggested that rain was on the way. Along here the thin coat of peat and soil that once covered the ground has been eroded to dust by years of walkers, exposing a gravelly subsoil that glittered with mica when the sun burst out from behind clouds and heated my face. Moments later the sun was banished as a sheet of misty rain pushed swiftly over the heather and enveloped me. I was too lazy to get on my waterproofs, believing it wouldn't last long, and for once, I was right; within minutes the squall of rain blew onwards towards the sea. As I continued, the warm wind, laden with heather perfumes, began to dry me.

There was a new skyline ahead now, green fields framed in darker hedgerows reaching to the rolling summits of Bray Head, Little Sugarloaf and Great Sugarloaf. But I had reached my planned farthest point south, and I turned and headed back on my homeward leg. Off to my left a grouse, heather-hidden, cackled like a *cailleach*, as the tors of Ticknock came into view, dwarfed by the towering gantries of telecommunication masts that signalled that I was back in the urban world. I was invigorated, renewed, inspired by my hour in the heather, but, as Lloyd Praeger wrote, 'It's a pity to leave the wilderness behind, and get back to the daily round.'

september

Colour flows from the woods, and the still air
Is musical with the cadence of the leaves
Singing as they fall.

– Brenda Murray Draper, 'Autumn'

Glendoher, 1 September

I'm a bit annoyed about our wood pigeons. They seem to have selected a particular branch in our birch to use as a toilet, and so the grass below this branch has become coated with their droppings. I'm not so concerned about the grass, but my youngest grandchildren play in the grass when they visit, and I have to cover up this latrine when they do.

We are, however, still very fond of the birds, and get great entertainment watching them in the garden. They may look tubby on the ground, but in flight they are the de Havilland Mosquito of birds, all speed and aerodynamic perfection. Wood pigeons mate for life, and can live up to sixteen years. They are a very successful species, and have become, in recent years, Ireland's most common large bird, equally at home in suburbia or the open countryside. Although they are joined in autumn by some migratory wood pigeons from Britain and northern Europe, our birds rarely stray far from where they hatched, and we are sure that the two we have been watching for the last few years are indeed our resident pair. They have an easy life, compared to many other birds. They are very fast feeders and only take 10 to 20 per cent of their time foraging and eating sufficient food for their day; they spend the rest of their time preening, flying about, and, in the case of the male anyway, chasing the female to mate. Although we particularly noticed our pairs mating in February, it seems that they continue with these activities well into the summer, having as many as three clutches in the year.

While wood pigeons are ordinary birds in many ways, the manner in which they feed their young is extraordinary. They are partial to a wide range of food, including wheat, oilseed rape, cauliflower, lettuce, radishes and peas, but when they are feeding their young, they refine whatever they are eating and convert it, in their crops, into a fat and vitamin-rich 'curd', which helps the young birds mature quickly. The only other birds that feed their young in this way are penguins and flamingos, so wood pigeons are members of a rather exclusive club.

Glendoher, 4 September

A flash of unfamiliar colour, a glimpse of carmine, lets us know this morning that one of our favourite birds, the goldfinch, is back in the garden. The group name for these beauties is a charm, a most appropriate term, and we always delight when a charm of goldfinches visits us, whether to enjoy the nyjer seeds we provide in our birdfeeders in Glendoher or the late summer thistles provided by nature in Kilcop. Although it is said that goldfinches are attracted to peanuts, we have not found that to be the case, and in recent years, to have any chance of seeing them in Glendoher, we have had to provide nyjer seeds. I was surprised to find, when I sought out information on the origin of these seeds, that they were the product of a plant called *Guizotia abyssinica*, grown as an edible oil crop in Ethiopia, and I presume the seeds we use have been flown the 5,000 kilometres from their country of origin. It was a reminder to me that globalism is all-pervasive, even in the seemingly simple matter of seed to feed birds in one's back garden. I'm afraid we are going to have to find an alternative for our goldfinches, maybe having to collect thistle seeds, because these

birds are best viewed perching on the fluffy tops of
tall thistles in autumn. They have a sharper beak
than their brother finches, designed for the delicate
job of extracting tiny seeds from thistles or teazels,
and a goldfinch working on the thistle head looks
as if it is puffing smoke as it discards the 'sails'. The
bird's Latin name is *Carduelis carduelis*, which must be
connected with the Latin name for thistle, which is
Carduus. Their folk name is also an appropriate one,
'Thistle-Tweaker'. A Christian legend recounts how
the goldfinch got the carmine face when one of them
plucked a thorn out of the crown of thorns Jesus was
wearing during his crucifixion, and a drop of blood
fell on him.

While some of our birds, such as the curlew
mentioned earlier, are endangered, the survival of the
goldfinch is remarkable. In the nineteenth century
catching and selling songbirds in cages was a major
industry to city dwellers, and one of the most sought-
after birds was the goldfinch. In one English town,
Worthing, in the year 1860, an astonishing 132,000
captured goldfinches are recorded as having been
sold. By 1903 the bird had become uncommon in
England when Helen Millman, suffragist and nature
writer, wrote in her book *Outside the Garden*:

A birdcatcher told me that in earlier years he
had on one occasion caught eleven dozen of
fine goldfinches in his net at one pull of the
string; now, however, in the same district,
with the help of bird-lime, he has to be
content with a few dozen during the whole
season ... The teazle, at one time regularly
cultivated, is now seldom seen even in the

wildest parts, and on the seed of the teazle the goldfinch used to feed largely ... The requirements of modern farming insist on the plough being driven close to the hedge, fields no longer go fallow, and thistles and other seed-bearing plants disappear. So, with the disappearance of his natural food, the Thistle-finch too is lost to us.

Walking along the banks of the Dodder in County Dublin in the 1970s, I came across a man in the process of catching birds to cage and sell. Thinking that I was curious about how he *caught* the birds, he went into a long explanation about them getting stuck on a sticky material that he had put on a branch, and that he sold them in a market in central Dublin. I was speechless, and so taken aback by what he was doing that I just passed on without comment. I doubt if the practice of catching birds for sale still continues, but although farming is even more intensive today than it was at the beginning of the twentieth century, the goldfinch has not only survived, it has made a great comeback. It is today regarded as a common bird, and, on occasions, autumn flocks of the bird can number in the thousands.

From our house in Glendoher we are blessed with the view we have out across the field to the Spinney at the far side. It is a longer view than most suburban gardens have, and from upstairs in the front of our house there is just a glimpse to be had of Cruagh Mountain, between the roofs of the houses to the south. I have been thinking for some time about this matter of a view, and the idea that one needs to live in a place that has some view out to the wider world.

Years ago we stayed in a house near Portmeirion on the Welsh coast; it had a grandstand, sweeping view that included mountain, sea, woods and shore. Our host was of the opinion that to live contentedly, one must be in a place that has, in view, a variety and depth of landscape, and plenty of sky: such a constant scene keeps one in touch with the wider world, it opens one up, and liberates one's soul. Everyone is different, however, and while I would have agreed with those sentiments, my paternal grandmother would have rejected them. In her later years my father used to bring her to our home every week for Sunday lunch; she didn't want to hurt his feelings, but she used to confide to me that she would prefer not to go, because there was nothing to see there but birds and trees! She was a town person, and enjoyed standing at her front door for hours daily, arms folded, overseeing her narrow street, greeting passersby and watching the world go by.

Kilcop, 7 September
Much to my surprise, I discovered today a fly agaric mushroom, complete with its white-spotted, shocking red caps, under the trees on the road side of the field. *Amanita muscaria*, to give it its proper name, is the typical fairy dwelling in children's books. Classed as inedible and poisonous, it has been used as a hallucinogenic drug in a lot of cultures, particularly in Asia, but it has also been used as an insecticide. Vikings are said to have chewed baked fly agaric mushrooms to prepare themselves for battle. One

Thrushes eggs in the woodpile on Hellfire Hill

The nestlings with their mother

Purple spires of loostrife

A seal at Dunmore East

A silverwashed fritilliary

A magpie moth in Gobbo's Garden

A red admiral on a buddleia globe

Cockleshells at Woodstown

As the leaves wither, the fraughans are at their best

Sparrowhawks in unison above the Spinney

A deer on Hellfire Hill

Redpolls feeding on nyjer seeds

The common garden spider

Golden autumn on
Hellfire Hill

A hungry blackbird

Fairy Castle cairn crusted with ice

wonders did Lewis Carroll experiment with the fungus: in *Alice's Adventures in Wonderland* he has the girl chewing a fly agaric mushroom to make herself bigger or smaller.

It seems to be a great autumn for fungi; great clusters of mushrooms, like fairies' hill-villages, crown the tree stumps that await being moved to Gobbo's Garden. Fungi might seem soft and delicate, but there are dozens of tiny parasols actually bursting through the hard-packed clay where the Kilcop driveway meets the road.

Because the weather conditions, both warmth and moisture, have been conducive to the growth of fungi, we took a trip out to the cliffs west of Dunmore. There, in former years, we picked great harvests of mushrooms in the fields overlooking the sea. We were disappointed this year; not a single one was found. A few huge horse mushrooms did appear in the 'lawn' in Kilcop, however, which we picked and simmered with milk and pepper and ate, but we found in the grass near the well two enormous puffballs, sitting side by side, the larger one nearly 150mm across, the smaller only a little less. When my daughter Fiona saw them she said that, from a distance, they looked like two great white skulls.

Harvesting 'country' mushrooms was as common as collecting blackberries when I was a child, but wild fungi have been eradicated in most agricultural land by the use of artificial fertilisers. The last great harvest our family had was in County Clare in the 1980s, when we collected two buckets full in an early morning hunt.

Traditionally, the only mushroom generally trusted to be safe to eat in rural Ireland was the common field mushroom. Perhaps we should educate ourselves on the many other fungi that thrive in Ireland: I have watched Eastern European immigrants quartering the ground under the coniferous trees on Hellfire Hill and filling sacks with delicious-looking fungi to bring home to cook.

Kilcop, 8 September

I had arranged for a man to come and help me with some fencing repairs at Kilcop, and he turned up today and began work early. He was a man who enjoyed talking as he worked, and he was full of stories of his home place, Mullinabroe in County Kilkenny, and its rich population of rural characters. He talked of one in particular who made a great impression on him when he was a boy. His name was Billie Lonergan, and although he originally came from Bunmahon in County Waterford, he had a small farm near Slieverue, County Kilkenny. Billie had no well on his farm and he had to go to the nearest 'pump' with ass and cart for water every day. These wells and pumps were great places for meeting people and hearing all the latest gossip, and young lads of the area used to hang about the pump in Mullinabroe just to hear Billie's stories.

One time he told them that, during the war, he was working in the fields when he heard a great bang on the hill, and when he hurried up there to investigate, he saw a German plane had crash-landed in a field. As he reached the plane, a door opened and twenty German stormtroopers poured out with their machine guns trained on Billie. They were just about to shoot when the sergeant leapt out after them and shouted 'Stop, don't fire, that's Billie Lonergan!' Anyway, Billie told his listeners that he had a look at the plane, and told the Germans to hang on while he got a few tools. He went home, got the necessary tools together and returned to the plane. He tinkered with the engines for a while, with the stormtroopers looking on, and in no time he had them working again. The sergeant thanked him with a box of German cigars and a bottle of schnapps; they all got in again, and flew away.

Another time Billie told the boys that he was crossing the bridge in Waterford City on his bike on the way home to Slieverue when he saw a man fall into the river. So he got off his bike, put it carefully against the wall, took off his overcoat, folded it and dived into the river. A crowd gathered on the shore to watch him save the man, whom he brought in to the quayside and gave up to those waiting. A member of the guards was minding his bicycle, but Billie shouted up to him that he was all wet, and he might as well swim the rest of the way home; would the guard hold on to the bike until he was next back in Waterford. I would hate to think that storytelling country characters such as Billie, like our insects, are becoming extinct.

Kilcop, 9 September
I spent the day thinning the branches of the trees we felled last year near Gobbo's Garden, and cutting them up into lengths for later sawing into logs. Most of the branch ends, too thin for useful firewood,

I wove into a dense matrix in the hedge where it is thin, and felt proud of myself to be usefully using every scrap of wood.

The following day I finished off what I had started, which included cutting down an ash tree ready for coppicing. It was a difficult one – because of the close proximity of other trees it wouldn't come down cleanly – so I had to call in a friend to help. With a rope tied high up on the trunk and lots of elbow grease, it still wouldn't fall because it was held up by adjacent branches, and try as we might we couldn't get it to budge. These kinds of circumstances can be dangerous if proper care is not taken, so, rather gingerly, we tried everything we could think of, falling flat on our backs and laughing hilariously at one stage when the rope gave way. Eventually, with the careful trimming of adjacent branches, we finally managed to fell the ash.

I also cut down one of the sitka spruces in the eastern end of the road hedge. It is one of a few I brought back as a seedling from the Slieve Blooms when I was there researching *Ireland's Waymarked Trails* in 1992. Early in my tree planting, I planted a few of these in the field, because sitka spruce are very fast-growing, but I have regretted doing so ever since. They are ugly trees, their firewood quality is poor, and they have little to recommend them.

It is a great time of the year to spend in Kilcop; the 'pressures' of summer, such as 'I must go for a swim' or 'I must go climbing in the Comeraghs' are entirely absent now. Although we do have our walks in Woodstown and Dunmore East, it's in a more relaxed way, and it's easy to stay put. The place is shaping up well, and I know, as usual, I won't get the year's work completed, but nothing is so urgent that it cannot be left to next year. My trimming work down in Gobbo's Garden has generated lots of timber lengths, which I'm now cutting into logs and stacking in the airing barn. The purchase of a new wheelbarrow has been a great boon – I cut the logs straight into it, and then wheel them to the barn and stack them.

Hellfire Hill, 11 September

I took a walk up Hellfire Hill today. After the steep and direct approach to the hilltop, which took me about fifteen minutes, I decided to take the long way around and so I descended steeply towards the north along a field fence. I spotted a bird on top of one of the dead trees to the west. I first thought it was a crow, but when I looked through the binoculars I saw that it was a sparrowhawk, big and bulky, and as I watched he flew up to a higher branch. He was a long way off but maybe I disturbed him, because he rose again shortly after and flew westwards, to finally alight on another tree a couple of hundred metres away. As I watched, a magpie alighted on the same tree, and hopped about, as if trying to annoy the sparrowhawk, but he didn't succeed. Then a blue jay came along and perched on the same spindly tree. With the three of them perched in the same tree, it would have been a great lineup if I had a camera with me. After a few minutes the magpie gave up his tormentations and flew off, followed a little later by the jay.

Along the track there was an extensive stand of thistles and a seed-rich herb called weld. Weld has tall spikes of yellow flowers in summertime, and was one of three main plants that were used as dyes in ancient

blue jay

times: madder was used for red, woad for blue, and
weld for yellow, and there is evidence of it being used
as far back as the Neolithic period. By September
each weld stalk is a spire of seeds that seed-eating
birds love, and sure enough, they were being grazed
by siskins and goldfinches as I approached, and
they all flew twittering away. Maybe this is what
the sparrowhawk was doing, waiting on the nearby
treetop to grab a siskin, and perhaps I disturbed his
breakfast. I also disturbed, trotted after and managed
to photograph with my iPhone a very pale painted
lady butterfly which was also feeding on the thistles.
Later I found a sparrowhawk's feather on the track, a
beautiful sliver of nature.

On the far side of the hill, at the side of the track,
there are stands of burdock every year at this time. It
is not a very common plant in this area. A member of
the highly successful thistle family, it spreads its seeds
by cleverly having them attached to minuscule hooks
or burrs, a natural Velcro, so every creature that

brushes close by cannot but take a few with it. The hooks are so efficient that they will even adhere to as smooth a surface as the palm of your hand. Burdock grows all over the world, and in Chinese medicine it is one of the foremost detoxifying herbs.

Along the way I caught the whiff of something dead wafting out from the trees. Years ago, when I first detected this unpleasant smell, I assumed that it came from some dead creature hidden in the trees, but later I discovered that it was the trademark of an unusual fungus, the stinkhorn, or *Phallus impudicus*. If you look under the trees, you can find the white shafts of these phallus-shaped mushrooms bursting through the debris on the forest floor. The conical cap is covered with a dark mass of spores that give off the carrion smell to attract flies and insects that help to disseminate its spores. It is just one of the many thousands of species of fungi that are to be found in Ireland; more, I believe, than all our plant species put together.

Fungi are an ancient race of organism that thrive beneath the ground. The mushroom seen above ground is only the fruit of the organism put up to spread its spores; the main part, or mycelium, remains below ground, and each one may measure many square metres. Indeed, many of these unseen organisms are vast. What is thought to be the largest organism in the world is a species of fungi discovered in Oregon in the United States which measured 9.6km^2 and is thought to be 8,000 years old. That's a long way from Hellfire Hill stinkhorns, but indicates that we still have a lot to learn about what is beneath the surface of the ground on which we walk.

Glendoher, 12 September

When I looked out the window early this morning, there was a heron perched on the side of our pond, feathers on his head standing up Mohican-like. He stood stock-still, his long, yellow dagger beak pointed down as he gazed into the water. It's not deep enough for the shubunkins to hide successfully, and I think I might have missed the heron swallowing them. Later, when I looked into the pond, I could see that one fish had survived the heron's visit. I think it was Fred, so I'm afraid that Flossy is no more. I had the pair of fish for only three months, and while I like the heron, I don't like it enough to feed it with expensive fish. Fred may be lonely but I don't think I will replace Flossy.

heron

The heron is a great survivor. Such a big bird must have provided great 'sport' in the past, particularly for hunters with guns during the nineteenth century, when anything that flew was fair game. Even though it was not so long ago, we would be horrified at the attitude to wildlife then. This passage from a tourist brochure entitled 'Guide to Tramore and Surrounding Scenery', published in 1858, gives a general idea of how people thought at the time:

> Fowl are to be met in plenty, the shooting at which affords good sport … Seagulls,

cormorants, murs, hagdowns, gannets, puffins, sea parrots, mother carey's chickens, blackdivers and ticklaces; and inshore about the rocks and islands wild pigeons, sealarks, curley, maybirds and Cornish daws. Rabbits, seals and otters are occasionally met with; and when fish are in plenty, gurnet, goat and mackerel playing over the water can be shot at in great numbers.

It is no wonder that many of these bird species are unknown today on our coasts! The heron is slow-flying and usually low-flying, and I'm sure they were a much-targeted bird.

Hellfire Hill, 13 September

I walked this morning in warm sunshine up Hellfire Hill. There was a coating of unexpected frost on the ground at the top. The new trees at the back are really coming on now, although phenomenal gorse growth has taken place this year. As I neared the south pond, I saw a young deer buck ahead, and I stopped still. He was nibbling grass at the side of the track, and he looked up and towards me as I stood there, motionless. He clearly saw me, but I was probably just another immobile feature in the landscape, so he dipped his head again and continued to nibble at the grass, nervously looking up a few times. He was beautiful, both delicate and athletically graceful on his slim legs, his coat glowing a chestnut colour in the sunlight. Then, without warning, he was spooked and leapt away, bounding a few metres down the track like a springbok and into the safety of the trees. Deer usually come down from the higher mountains to the foothills in winter, no doubt to avail of the warmer temperatures nearer the city, brought about by the heat generated by three quarters of a million people and their lifestyles. I usually see deer on Hellfire Hill from the end of October, but this young male was early.

The south pond was very low, and no work had been done to protect it after I had brought it to Coillte's attention yet again. In spite of low water, pond skaters still dimpled the water as they slid across the mirrored sky, shining whirligig beetles tirelessly circled each other and metallic blue dragonflies flitted to and fro.

The limited numbers of amphibians we have in Ireland are decreasing alarmingly, partly because their habitats, like this little water world, are disappearing. Not so long ago ponds were common in the countryside, and every farm had at least one for their livestock. Today, water for animals is usually piped into troughs, and there is no further need for ponds, so we have to protect and preserve what we have left of these small, but important ecosystems. It is such a pity that what remains of the south pond, after Coillte's works in the area, provides such a limited habitat.

The noble firs on the hill are showing an amazing growth of their fat, vertical cones; each one, I have discovered, may contain up to a thousand seeds. Red squirrels must be active on the western side of the hill, because the upright cones of the noble firs have been well grazed, with, in places, only their little toadstool-shaped stumps remaining on high branches. To get at these, a squirrel has to climb to the top of the tree and expose itself in the clear air to the danger of predators such as sparrowhawks or peregrines.

Red squirrels disappeared from Hellfire Hill two or three decades ago, but are now returning. A couple of years ago I had been heaving my way up the steep way to the top of the hill when the concentrated chirping of lots of birds drew my attention to the treetops. I looked up just in time to see a flock of finches roller-coasting along through the larches and out of sight. But then something else caught my eye: a squirrel perched in the nearest tree, but a squirrel with a profile that I was no longer accustomed to. It had long ears, and a long bushy tail. I had my binoculars with me and I soon had him in focus – yes, it was a red squirrel, his rusty chestnut coat glowing in the low sun. While I was thinking this is marvellous, but one squirrel doesn't necessarily mean that the little animals are returning, and it would hardly be worth my while reporting it to Michael Viney, another red appeared and made my day. They both were foraging among the larch cones, checking them all and then plucking ones that were to their liking, and chewing them. *Mirabile dictu*, it was the first time I had seen red squirrels on Hellfire Hill for more than twenty years.

I carried on to the top of the hill from where the Mournes were a golden-pink apparition on the northern horizon, catching patches of morning sun on their eastern flanks like watercolour brushstrokes and contrasting with a dark, glowering sky.

I walked on westwards down the other side of the hill to where, beyond the white dome of Piperstown Hill, the frost-covered western summits were in view, soaking in the sunlight.

This is a great time of year for seeing the birds return to centre stage. Great flocks of finches flowed noisily from tree to tree, and I was surprised to see that there were also very early flocks of fieldfares 'racheting' along, chasing one another and feeding on bright orange rowan berries. Clumps of dying thistles along the track were decorated with tortoiseshells and red admirals, basking in the warmth of the sun after a cold night.

As I followed the track around towards the east again, I paused to watch a dogfight between a sparrowhawk, two gulls and a grey-backed crow. The battle began with the crow harassing two juvenile hawks, drawing the attention of an adult hawk which, protecting its young, immediately attacked the crow. After a short scrap, the crow was driven off, and the hawk then turned on two gulls, which had been innocently passing on their way west. As the three birds wheeled and circled around each other, the gulls squealing, the crow returned to the fray. After some spectacular aerobatics, the hawk must have reckoned that the odds were too great, and, tucking in its wings, it hurtled down to cover in the conifers.

On my way back down the hill, I came upon the location where I had seen the squirrels earlier and, really not expecting anything, had a look to see if they were still there. Almost immediately I caught sight of one, and then the other, still foraging. But as I watched, I saw that there were five squirrels there. Some of them looked a little smaller and I wondered if it might be a family group. I examined the ground carefully and, sure enough, soon found the little remains of what they had eaten, cone stalks stripped of their seeds. I continued on my way, elated at what I had seen!

Glendoher, 24 September

For some years I have been puzzled by finding, in the front and back gardens, the remains of walnuts, sometimes in their shells, sometimes still partially complete in their soft outer covering. Neither I nor my neighbours have a walnut tree, so it was a great mystery. Today, however, I saw some rooks moving very actively in a tree behind the apartments, and one of them took off and flew over the house going south, with two globular 'things' in his widely opened beak. At first I thought they were chestnuts, and then it dawned on me. The tree at the back of the apartments must be a walnut tree, and this is where the walnuts came from. Sometimes, a rook would take what my mother used to call a 'lazy man's load', too much to safely carry, resulting in nuts being dropped in transit into the garden. Some bird species are known to deliberately drop from a height foodstuffs that need to be broken open, such as nuts or bones, to retrieve marrow, but in this case I believe it was purely accidental.

Glendoher, 26 September

The solution to the walnut mystery was confirmed this morning as I stood in the sunlit garden, my back to the warmth, just absorbing the smells on the clean air and resisting the urge to get gloves on and weed the nettles. There was a constant stream of rooks bearing walnuts making a beeline over the house from the walnut tree. As I watched, I even saw a couple of them alighting on my chimney and, harried by squawking magpies, starting to crack open the tough walnut shells.

Although spiders are plentiful in the garden all summer long, I notice their webs more often in the autumn. The most visible and fascinating webs belong to the *Araneus*, or common garden spider, which weaves the typical spider's web, an intricate oval orb web. I have only once had the good fortune to watch the building of an orb web, and it was a most rewarding and fascinating experience. Unfortunately, I missed the first steps, where the spider, having decided on an ideal location to place its web, casts the first thread onto the breeze so that it crosses the space where the web will be and adheres to a leaf or a branch on the far side. After reeling in this thread and tightening it, the spider walks across it to the centre and begins to construct the radials of the web; this is where what was going on came to my attention while I was checking for slug damage on our lupins. I watched as the spider, in a kind of dance, swung to and fro, spinning silk from its tail, and when the radials were completed, it began to move spirally out from the centre with the circular threads, attaching them, as it went, to the radials. Then beginning from the outside, the amazing creature retraced its 'steps', moving in towards the centre, but this time it was laying down sticky threads, the ones that would trap its prey. It all took about twenty or thirty minutes, and when the web was finished, the spider settled at a location at the side of the web, hidden by a leaf. Some orb spiders sit at the centre of the web, but this one, perhaps wary of becoming preyed upon itself, by birds, was being careful. There it waited, one foot on a non-adhesive thread connected to the entire network, so that once prey landed in the web, it would immediately know, and would race out and pounce upon it. I didn't wait to see the first visitor to the web, and left wondering how I could get the spider to become interested in slugs.

For the rest of the day I noticed many tiny spiders, voyaging across the garden on their long glistening gossamer sails.

Glendoher, 28 September

In the spider's web this morning I found the remains of a crane fly, tightly bound up in silk, hanging in the orb web. It would have given the spider a good feed, and has saved our garden from the attentions of a leatherjacket. The crane fly – what we used to call, as children, 'daddy-long-legs' – looks a bit ridiculous with its long, segmented body and very long legs, but it is well designed for the environment it lives in. One cannot imagine a better way for an insect to negotiate grassland than to have long legs, which in this case make it possible for the creature to walk on the tops of blades of grass. The same long legs keep the female's body in a vertical position when laying eggs, which it does by bobbing up and down, depositing eggs in soft soil at every bob. The eggs hatch into the larvae called leatherjackets in the spring, just in time to benefit from the spring growth of grass and plants. But for the incessant labour of rooks, starlings and other birds, and indeed spiders, these larvae could devastate large areas of grassland.

October

Across the land a faint blue veil of mist
Seems hung; the woods wear yet arrayment sober
Till frost shall make them flame …

– Siegfried Sassoon, 'October'

murmuration

SEPTEMBER SIDLED SEAMLESSLY INTO
October, when 'scarlet fruits the russet hedge
adorn'. As its name hints, it was, in the ancient
Roman calendar, the eighth month of a year in
which winter was a monthless period: January and
February are said to have been inserted around 700
BC. October is the month when remaining butterflies
are partying wildly, knowing the end is nigh; on the
nearby hills clouds of small whites, painted ladies,
red admirals, tortoiseshells and peacocks graze on
the last of the thistles and ragwort that are bursting
through heather and gorse. The last few swallows
quarter the skies, dipping to and fro, skimming the
heather moorland, stocking up on food for their
great exodus.

Glendoher, 7 October

The return of blue tits to the garden, flitting busily
from tree to bush after a long summer absence,
is a lovely sight. A mixed flock of finches passed
through the garden this morning, greenfinches and
chaffinches in a communal search for food. There
were about thirty birds in all, and they cascaded over
the wall into the garden, spent a minute or two in
the birch, and then, as if on command, flowed over
the back wall into the field. Now that the autumn is
here, it is clear that birds are enjoying the freedom
of not having nests to build, territories to defend,
or broods to feed. Their only need now is to feed up
well to survive the winter. October is the time when,
rather than rail at one another, birds travel about
and feed together, sociably, and, it often appears to
me, gossip. Some birds, such as the long-tailed tit
and the goldfinch, will flock throughout the year,
while robins and wrens do not have any interest in
socialising at any time with birds other than their own
family. Moving along in flocks allows birds to feed
well; the more birds in the flock, the more there are
to search for suitable food sources, and while feeding,
a bird in a flock can spend less time keeping an eye
out for predators. Hierarchies, however, are always
in force: in flocks of wood pigeons that one sees in
grassy swards in parks at this time of year, it is very
likely that the dominant birds will be found in the
middle of the crowd while the weaker birds are left on
the margins, where they are more vulnerable.

Perhaps the most noticeable autumn aerial
gatherings, or murmurations, are flocks of starlings.
I have been lucky enough to see these tight formations
of starlings, over fifty or so, sweeping and flowing

across the sky in breathtaking, shape-shifting patterns. There are, however, places around the country where one can see thousands of these busy little birds formatting together in the evening, before they descend to roost in trees. While it is clear that predators would have a difficult time targeting one bird in these hypnotic gyrations, there must be a stronger reason for them to do it. In spite of the great leaps in knowledge in the past century, about our galaxy and about the universe on the one hand, and the microscopic world on the other, many more ordinary mysteries of everyday nature remain.

Ticknock, 10 October

The wind was icy today, and as I came out of the woods at Ticknock, I spotted a bird about fifty metres away which I thought was a grouse, in the heather to the side of the track. It was precisely the same autumn colour as the heather, and I wouldn't have seen it except that its silhouette against the sky caught my eye. I walked towards it for about thirty metres, and then stood still for a few minutes. The bird looked about a little, but didn't seem bothered by my presence, or else hadn't spotted me. I walked slowly towards it again, and when I got to within ten metres I reckoned that it was a golden plover. I had seen a flock of these on Ticknock in April, and as I was wondering what the bird was doing here on its own, it suddenly took off with a warning squeal, followed by about forty other golden plovers, which had presumably been foraging away out of my sight behind a hummock of heather. They swept into the sky to wheel and turn in formation, like a murmuration of starlings, and then swung back over my head and disappeared off behind the hill in a wonderful swirling movement.

Glendoher, 14 October

Our two-year-old grandson, Sam, came to visit us today, and, as always when the weather is good, we went out into the garden seeking out garden insects, what he calls 'creatures'. He enjoys watching the bumblebees foraging for the last of this year's nectar in the remaining flowers, and looking under flowerpots and flat stones where woodlice are usually gathered in abundance. The woodlice scatter in a slow grey explosion when exposed, seeking cover, and Sam's eyes widen with amazement. Today, in the midst of the woodlice was a golden centipede, which swiftly and sinuously disappeared under the nearest leaf. A few weeks ago, Sam, who has learned to search carefully for new 'creatures', spotted, with great excitement, a crane fly perched on its spindly legs in the grass. When I was a child, my father, who was a keen gardener, hated these insects, which we called 'daddy-long-legs'. For Sam, it was just a new 'creature', and one with wings at that. Bees do not stay still long enough for him to observe their wings, but those on the crane fly are obvious, long and glistening. Sam cannot pronounce the letter 'L' yet, and so he calls this new creature 'Daddy Ronregs'.

Glendoher, 16 October

Our shrubs are hanging down with berries after the good summer, and birds are queuing up to feast on them. The red and yellow berries on the pyracantha are widely enjoyed, and I have seen many species, from blackbird to wood pigeon, stripping branches. In a few weeks we will have purple berries on the berberis that will appeal to blackbirds and thrushes. If there are any left towards winter they will be eaten by grateful visiting redwings or fieldfares. Berries are high in carbohydrates, but birds cannot rely on carbohydrates alone and so they will have to augment their diet with protein, which they will get in the insects and worms they find.

Birds have a symbiotic relationship with the shrubs that they feed on. They need the food provided by berries, and berry-bearing shrubs want to broadcast their seed as far as possible. When most birds eat a berry, they digest the pulp and eject the seed in their faeces, so the seed reaches the ground with a surrounding of lime-rich material that helps it grow when it germinates. Some birds, however, abuse the neat bird/bush system and break the rules; wood pigeons, finches and tits will chew away the pulp to get at the seeds, and then will eat them; these are, after all, more nutritious than the berries.

Ticknock, 18 October

I am enjoying a welcome hiatus in book and magazine article work which allows me to take a morning walk up Ticknock without feeling guilty. The air this morning was no longer full of swallows twittering. They have all gone south, but their joyous songs were replaced by the harsh warning call of a stonechat, perched on a post, rasping under a bright blue sky. I reminded myself that the blue is not the colour of the sky, it is the colour of nothing, of emptiness, of

space. Or so they say, and gazing up into space, part
of me rejected, out of hand, the hard scientific fact of
the matter; I prefer the idea that the sky is blue.

Dublin Bay was laid out sharp and clear between
the bookends of Howth and Dún Laoghaire Pier, and
out to sea, an armada of creamy white sails hung in a
line stretching to the Baily Bank Lighthouse, looking
like a Viking fleet awaiting a signal to invade.

It was brilliantly sunny at the Fairy Castle, and I
didn't delay long. Dazzled by the sun's reflection in
the pools left by the previous night's rain, I headed
southwards along the waterlogged path that follows
an ancient mearing ditch. A few hundred metres
farther on, at an eroded granite tor, I stopped and
sat on a throne of stone and surveyed the vista of
Glencullen valley laid out below. There was a time,
not so long ago, when I might have been asked at a
dinner party what I had been up to that day, to be
met by blank expressions when I'd reply that I was
walking in the mountains. I could see that the dinner
guests found it difficult to frame what was for them
the obvious follow-up question, 'Why?' While times
have changed, and hill-walking is today a very popular
activity for young and old, I still meet people who
are a tad suspicious about the activity, and who might
tentatively ask me about it, as if they believe it to be
a most strenuous penance rather than an enjoyable
activity. For most people, however, apart from those
stalwarts who insist on bagging as many peaks as they
can in a day, hill-walking can be an easy-going and
sociable activity that exchanges the tarmac, concrete
and glass of the city for natural soul-soothing
surroundings, where Brexit and Trump matters
fade away. Although I have been walking around

Ticknock for many years, the huge increase in walkers there, owing mainly to the fine paths that have been constructed, can only be good, particularly if it helps to introduce more of our urban populace to the wonders of nature, and maybe encourages them to be concerned enough to help prevent the destruction of what is left of it. Unless you are unfortunately unhealthy, or a century old, there is no reason why you couldn't walk up to the Fairy Castle and onwards to sit on a granite tor and gaze into the valley of Glencullen.

As I sat there, a red grouse, which must have frozen in its place in the nearby heather when I turned up, eventually lost its nerve and took off with a loud flapping of wings. It cackled loudly as it flew downhill, just skimming the heather, with the sun reflecting off its chestnut-brown back.

On my way back, I came out of the trees onto the track heading north, and before me, not more than twenty metres away, I saw a small herd of deer, one of them a young stag. I stopped still and watched. The stag had noticed me, and he turned to face me, his back turned to his little herd of females. When stags do this, they flare the white fur on their behinds to signal danger to the deer behind them. At this, the rest of the little herd nervously moved off. The stag faced me, fearlessly, with big, dark eyes and eight points to his antlers, which suggested he might be between eight and twelve years old. After a long pause, enough to scrutinise me thoroughly and make it clear that he didn't welcome my presence, he turned and haughtily and unhurriedly followed his harem, head in the air. Although it was only October, they were already in their dark grey-brown winter coats,

excellent camouflage against the dull background,
except for their white tails brightly bobbing, as
they descended into the trees. I feel extraordinarily
fortunate that I can frequently see these magnificent
wild animals so close to my suburban home; it's such
a thrill. Usually, if you come near to a herd of deer
in the hills, the first you may know of their presence,
because of their extraordinarily effective camouflage,
is the strong, whistle-like warning call of their
guardian stag.

These were either sika deer, or a hybrid, the result
of sika interbreeding with native red deer. I think you
would have to be an expert to identify which is which
in the Dublin and Wicklow Mountains. Sika were
introduced into County Wicklow from Japan by Lord
Powerscourt in the middle of the nineteenth century;
up until then, native red deer ruled the hills, but
it is possible that there are no pure red deer left in
Wicklow today.

The rut must be over in this part of the hills: the
young stag I met had clearly won this little harem. I
have never experienced the battles of the rut in the
mountains, but if one wants to see this extraordinary
primal activity, the Phoenix Park in Dublin is the
place to go. I have watched rutting males there
battling it out, noisily crashing into each other
again and again, until one of them gives in. One has
to be careful not to get too near; deer in the park
will normally move away on the close approach of
humans, but during the rut there is nothing in the
minds of the pair fighting other than overcoming
their opponent, and it can be dangerous to get in the
way. I once had to make a very quick and ignominious
retreat when I was photographing a rut.

Glendoher, 21 October

On a brief walk this morning up and through St
Enda's Park, I was fortunate to observe the cruel
reality of everyday nature when I saw a hawk take
down a wood pigeon. I was walking along the edge
of the playing fields when two birds burst out of
the trees at speed, close together, both banking,
twisting, just above head height and no more than five
metres away from me. As they flew by, I saw that one
was a wood pigeon, and the other a hawk that kept
clutching at the pigeon with its talons. As they passed
me, the hawk got a firm grip on its prey, after which
they tumbled together to the ground, under a tree
about eight metres away.

If I had had a camera, I would have had got a
remarkable picture of the pigeon lying on the ground,
already dead I believe, with the hawk standing over
it, straddling its body. What surprised me was there
seemed to be no *coup de grâce*, as such, by the hawk;
it seems that the pigeon was furiously flying one
moment, and dead a second later as it hit the ground.
The hawk was initially nervous about me being so
close; it stood erect and fixed me with its cruel golden
eyes. I stood stock-still, not looking directly at the
birds, but watching the hawk out of the corner of
my eye. After less than a minute it decided that I
was not a threat, and, positioning itself, long yellow
legs braced, it began quickly plucking the pigeon's
feathers. The hawk would duck its head, pluck a small
bunch of feathers with its hooked beak, then, raising
its head, seemed almost to puff them away, before
ducking down to the task once more.

Meanwhile, within a minute of the coming to earth
of the two birds, an assembly of magpies gathered in

the trees above them from all corners of the park and started a loud haranguing in their usual raucous way. How do they sense, so fast, that something is up, and head for the scene of the crime? None of them came near to the hawk, which ignored them. It continued to pluck, raising its head frequently and glancing around watching for threats. Then, not happy with its exposure, it began to drag the pigeon into better cover. There the work continued, until, still not satisfied, the hawk picked up the limp dead pigeon and flew with it, a metre or two above the ground and seemingly effortlessly, across the avenue leading up to St Enda's, and into the cover of the trees on the far side. I followed, and came quite close to it in its new location. Although it had the cover of plenty of branches and leaves above it, I could clearly see it, and after nervously looking about for a couple of minutes, it started plucking again. The magpies had also followed, but because their quarry was hidden from them in the undergrowth, they soon gave up and flew away. The hawk, meanwhile, had plucked the breast of the pigeon, and began to tear flesh. It ate fast, sometimes pulling long stringy bits, at other times pecking at some choice bloody piece.

I decided to leave it to it, and walked away. I had never seen a hawk kill another bird before, and I was very impressed. When I got home, I looked up the characteristics of the bird I had seen, a light grey breast up to its chin, and dark back, yellow legs with the tops covered with 'trousers'. Its size, about the same length as the pigeon, suggested a sparrowhawk rather than a kestrel or a merlin, and its plumage indicated a female.

Glendoher, 26 October

It has been a week of brilliant, unexpected autumn
glory. The sky is powder blue, without a cloud, but
it's breezy today, and gales are promised for later.
The trees all around, and the roofs of the apartments
next door where the can be seen through the foliage,
are drenched with the brightest sunlight and cast
deep pockets of shade. Autumn is running late: this
close to the first of November, it is unusual to see
that leaves are still on most of the trees, and only
beginning to tend towards their glorious russet
shades. Even if one were to ignore the rest of our
local nature and concentrate just on the trees that
can be seen from our back window, there is plenty of
interest to observe.

The farthest trees visible from the window are a
pair of willows. They are too far away to identify the
precise species, but they are swaying heavily today,
undulating in the breeze, bending over and back
ponderously, their slight upper branches laden down
with a better than usual crop of leaves and catkins.
Unlike many of the trees I can see from my window,
the willow is a native tree, and Irish folklore is full
of references to and stories about the tree. The Irish
harp was traditionally made from willow, and perhaps
the most famous harp, Brian Boru's instrument kept
in Trinity College, Dublin, is made entirely from the
wood of the willow.

The willows look almost juvenile in comparison
with their neighbour, the old walnut tree I have
become aware of only recently. Today its large, floppy
leaves are looking tired: some are still grey-green,
others look crispy, browny-gold, and the rest are
the many shades in between. Unlike the willow, the

walnut has strong, firm upper branches which limit its movement in reaction to the breeze to a frenzied trembling amongst the leaves.

Behind the old walnut, and only barely visible from here, is what I think might be a cedar, possibly a Lebanon cedar, with long, upward-angled branches. It would be an unusual tree for this area; it may have been planted by the painter Seán Keating.

Now a series of white puffy clouds is moving quickly across the sky from the south-west, thickening as it reaches the eastern horizon. The wind is increasing, and although these new clouds are not scudding across the sky, they are moving with intent, almost as fast as a lone seagull that flashed past, high up, riding the gusts.

The tree that dominates the outlook from the back window is our Himalayan birch. It is an aristocratic birch, and a beauty, with a gleaming white bark that peels away to reveal the next layer as warmly golden. Its translucent greenery allows the sun to penetrate and reflect brightly off the bark, and even in dull weather it shines out, so it is always a cheerful tree to behold. Its leaves are a blend of bright yellow and blue-green, and are beginning to drop now: soon our back garden will be clothed in a yellow crunchy carpet. We often stuff the leaves into black plastic bags with some water, and stow them away for a few years. The first time we did this, on the advice of a friend, we were astonished when we opened the bags after three years to find that the leaves had broken down into beautiful dark clay. Mulch of this sort improves the quality of soil, and we spread it in pots, containers and on flowerbeds.

We have gained pleasure without measure gazing out at the beech trees of the Spinney over the years during breakfast, lunch and dinner. At this time of the year it is particularly beautiful, and there is always something happening there. Whether it is observing the antics of the flocks of magpies skipping from branch to branch and trying to dislodge the sparrowhawk, or the wood pigeons perched in the top branches to catch the morning sun, or just enjoying the constant season clock that big deciduous trees are, the Spinney gives us year-long entertainment and opportunities for contemplation. There are lots more trees I can glimpse from here, but even limiting it to those mentioned above provides so many layers of information to explore: for instance, what is their natural history, and how did those that are not native get here?

The walnut tree has a particularly interesting back story. It is a native of Asia Minor, and it has been grown as an orchard tree since the time of the Ancient Greeks. The experts cannot agree on when the tree came west to these islands; some say it was brought to Britain by the Romans; its botanical name, *Juglans regia*, is translated as 'the royal nut of the god Jove'. The Saxons knew the tree and called it the 'welsh nut tree', welsh in this instance meaning strange or foreign. The tree was probably brought to Ireland from England during the Elizabethan period. In Ireland, grown from a nut, the tree will rarely produce a nut harvest, but some horticulturalists have had great success by using grafting techniques, and I understand that at least one Wicklow farm is producing walnuts commercially. It is a very useful food; the walnut is one of the most nutritious nuts, containing 15 to 25 per cent protein, and high levels of Omega 3.

The willows I can see are one of the 500 varieties of the tree catalogued worldwide, of which we in Ireland have about twenty. Together with the juniper, they were amongst the first trees to clothe the landscape of Ireland in the wake of the receding glaciers of the last Ice Age, and they can vary from tall, stately trees to low shrubs.

The cedar of Lebanon, if that is indeed what can be seen from the window, also has a long and interesting history. It originated in Lebanon, Syria and Turkey, and the Bible mentions Solomon employing tens of thousands of slaves to fell cedars in order to build his temple.

As for the magnificent beeches of the Spinney, according to pollen records the beech may have been established in Ireland some thousands of years ago, but the first record of planting the tree notes that it took place at Shelton Abbey in County Wicklow in the seventeenth century. Today the beech makes up some of the finest stretches of woodland in the country, and while there are not many nature records held by Ireland, the largest planted beechwood in Europe is Mullaghmeen Forest in County Westmeath.

Glendoher, 29 October
It is turning out to be yet another wonderfully warm autumn, which is tricking many plants, such as our primroses, into thinking that spring has arrived already. The trees are giving up their fruits, and acorns, beech mast and chestnuts are everywhere on the ground in Marlay Park. The other day I saw rooks

harvesting acorns: the nut is a high-energy food, and one acorn is apparently equal to a dozen earthworms. I understand that blue tits, usually insect eaters, are very partial to beech mast in wintertime. As a child, walking home from school on autumn days, my friends and I used to break open the neat, shiny triangular cases of the mast to release the little nuts which we used to chew. I was surprised recently to read that beech mast in quantity can be toxic, leading to 'severe abdominal pain, nausea and diarrhoea'; we never experienced this, but then we didn't eat more than one or two nuts at a time. In Germany during the Second World War, beech mast was roasted, ground and used as a coffee substitute, and rural children were given the task of collecting the nuts and taking them to be crushed in communal mills to produce an oil similar to olive oil, for use in cooking and with salads.

wood pigeon

November

But of all the months when earth is greener
Not one has clean skies that are cleaner,
Clean and clear and sweet and cold,
They shine above the earth so old …

– Edward Thomas, 'November'

blackthorn

Glendoher, 1 November

Edward Thomas's clear, clean skies are what make, for me, November the best month for landscape photography: its only shortcoming is the brief few hours of good daylight.

Soon temperatures will begin to drop as we slide into winter, and so today we re-erected our bird feeders, taken down a few months ago, on a pole just outside the kitchen window. These feeders will give us a glorious grandstand view, from our kitchen, of the colourful avian winter visitors that we can expect over the next few weeks. Our own local birds benefit, of course, and great tits, blue tits and coal tits are our most common customers. The Himalayan birch in our back garden constantly attracts the tits, because its easily peeled bark provides ease of access to all those tiny creatures, invisible to me, that inhabit the tree. The little birds forage tirelessly and speedily through the branches, hanging this way and that, getting their fill. Their visits to the peanut feeder are in–out; they queue up in the birch or in the cherry tree next door, and when their turn comes, they dart down, perch, look all around for any sign of predators, grab a nut, and are off again.

The peanuts also attract blackcaps at this time of the year, although the female, with her nice brown cap, seems to be less shy about approaching the feeder than the male. The blackcap is normally a summer visitor to Ireland, departing when the summer ends for Iberia or North Africa, but some of them over-winter here, particularly on the east coast. Ours might also be from the central European population, having come west and south to the mildness of the Atlantic to spend the winter in Ireland. Greenfinches and siskins are other winter visitors to our garden, some of which have also travelled from central Europe. We put out mixed seeds, which sometimes get their attention, but at other times this offering seems to be ignored by all except the tubby wood pigeons that patrol the ground under the feeders, enjoying the scraps from the table. We have been using nyjer seeds to attract goldfinches and redpolls, but there must be something more sustainable we can use.

As soon as we re-establish the bird feeders, however, our local grey squirrels turn up. They have been about all year, and frequently pass through the garden on their way to some other domain, but as soon as the feeders are out, they are daily visitors, often two at a time. Grey squirrels have been part of our local fauna in Glendoher for only about a dozen years, but they seem to have multiplied.

There were no squirrels in Waterford when I was

growing up; I saw my first wild squirrel in the 1970s, in woodland in the Dublin Mountains, and it was a red. I was thrilled at this first sighting, but the animal was very shy and I couldn't get near enough to it to photograph it. I went back to the same place a week later with a borrowed telephoto lense on my camera. The squirrel was kind enough to turn up again, this time with a friend, and I got a few shots as they foraged along the ground. The bright red/brown of the animal's fur stood out strongly against the greenery of the woodland floor, and I wasn't surprised to learn later that reds do not normally spend much time on the ground. When these two spotted me, they darted for the nearest tree and ascended it on the other side, out of my sight. I stood still, hoping to get another glimpse. After a few moments, one of them peeked around the tree at me, from about three metres up. I stood absolutely still and was amazed, after he decided, because of my stillness, that I was not really there, when he descended again and continued to forage on the ground. His companion also peeked around the trunk, but was not as convinced, and disappeared into the canopy. I continued to be a statue, but as soon as I raised my camera, the squirrel on the ground was gone like a flash.

I would have preferred to see red squirrels in our garden, but I was also thrilled when greys began to appear there. It was wonderful to see these little animals springing along, bushy tails in the air, stopping and sitting upright as they looked around. Greys are not native but are certainly prolific; all the greys in Ireland are descendants of six pairs that were a wedding present for a bride in Castleforbes, County Longford in 1911.

The red squirrel, with its colouring, bushy tail and long tufts rising from its ears, is an attractive animal, while the grey, let's face it, looks a bit like a large rat with a fancy tail. But it is such a fearless and determined animal, going to extraordinary lengths to get at the birds' nuts in our garden, that one cannot help but admire it, and we greatly enjoy watching its antics. In the beginning, concerned that not only would they frighten off the birds, but also quickly finish off the food, I tried to find ways to prevent them reaching the feeders. They made short work of plastic nut containers, biting through them and causing the nuts to cascade onto the ground, where they could feed at their leisure. The replacement steel wire containers were no better; somehow, they just chewed through the steel. Greasing the pole from which the containers are hung with Vaseline made no difference: if they found it too slippery, they just performed a spectacular jump up onto the container, and, hanging upside down in a most comical way, proceeded to feed. Now and then the animal would lose its grip and fall to the ground, but, undeterred, it was quickly up again. I even rigged up a lampshade on the pole, which I was sure the animal would not be able to bypass, but after a few attempts, the lampshade was conquered. In the end I surrendered and let nature take its course; the squirrel was a part of the everyday garden, and there was nothing I could do. Although I believe they have their drey, or nest, in the Spinney, the grey squirrels have made themselves at home in our garden, and now we just watch them with interest and amusement.

We have even seen pairs of squirrels mating in the garden. The gestation period is a short forty-four days, and the average litter size is three, so they must be multiplying at a considerable rate.

Ticknock, 2 November
I made my way up to Ticknock at half past eight this morning; it was a clear sunny day after one of the first frosty nights of the season. Slieve Gullion, Slieve Foy and the individual peaks of the Mournes – particularly the bare, conical Donard – were easy to identify. Patches of mist rising from declivities in the forestry were spectacularly pierced by early sunbeams. Approaching the Fairy Castle, I saw a raven rise up from the cairn. He took off vertically and hovered on the stiff westerly breeze, honking gently. It was plain that he was not afraid of me, just being a little discommoded, and he moved off a short distance and landed again. Maybe it was the quality of the morning light, but he seemed really large, particularly when I was sitting on the cairn and he took off and drifted low over my head, effortlessly hanging on the wind.

I searched the eastern horizon, as I always do here, and sure enough, the grey mounds of Holyhead Mountain and, farther south, Snowdonia, were peeping up from beyond the Irish Sea. Reluctantly, I handed back my seat to the raven and made my way south-east towards Two Rock. On the way, I decided to cut across the heather to intercept the track back to the east. Halfway across, I put up a half-dozen curlews, a bird I had never seen on Ticknock, and the long-beaked beauties squealed protests as they rose and scattered. The haunting 'courliii' cry of the bird was once commonly heard in the Irish countryside, but it is said to be a threatened species now, with numbers in Ireland reduced to under 200 breeding pairs, so this was a lucky sighting.

Glendoher, 6 November

The grey squirrel has gone up again in my estimation. Apart from the feeders we have outside the kitchen window, we have a couple of others in the garden, and one that is hung on a very long string from a branch of our birch, to deny the squirrel access. This morning I was amused to watch a squirrel climb the tree, eyeing the feeder on the long string. It went out along the branch and cocked its head, looking down at the feast of peanuts. Then it looked down the other side of the branch. I was smiling, and saying under my breath, 'That's a difficult one for you,' when the animal began to do something I did not believe it had the brainpower to accomplish. It began to haul the feeder up by the string, 'hand over hand', until it got it to the branch, and, clamping the string to the branch with one paw, it reached down and brought the whole feeder up onto the branch and began to enjoy its breakfast. I was astonished. I had heard of rooks doing something like this, and rooks are clever and resourceful creatures, but I didn't think squirrels were that smart. Outwitted again!

Glendoher, 15 November

Spiders are on the move this morning, signalled
by many loops of shining gossamer across the back
garden. October and November are the months for
tiny spiders, so-called 'money spiders', to move to
new pastures by taking to the air in huge numbers,
almost always invisibly. Sometimes, however, if you
are in the right place as the sun is beginning to set,
their numbers and the beauty of their voyaging is
plain to see.

Some years ago I was fortunate to be in such a
right place at the right time. I was taking a walk in
the Phoenix Park on a November afternoon, when I
noticed the low sun was gleaming off the grass a few
hundred metres away, as if the sward was waterlogged
or had standing water on it as after a heavy shower.
But as I looked more closely at the ground near me,
I could see that the light was not reflecting off water,
but on myriads of spiders' webs that seemed, from
where I stood, to be crossing at right angles to the line
between the sun and me. Nearer to me, the individual
strands were clearly visible, shimmering and waving
in the light breeze like a seascape in moonlight. What
was truly amazing was, as I walked on, the entire park,
including under copses of trees, seemed to be covered
with this gossamer mantle. I could see new lengths of
web drifting in the evening air a metre or more above
the ground and dropping to join the others when a
trailing end snagged a blade of grass. I was a fortunate
observer of the migration of millions of spiders, a
witness to a wonderful show of aeronautical magic.

I had thought that they were all 'baby' spiders,
but these movements include both spiderlings and
mature spiders of a variety of species. In France their

gossamer web is called 'virgin's thread'. It happens
only when there is a very light breeze, but the earth's
static electricity field may also help: the spider climbs
up to the top of, say, a blade of grass, and casts up
into the air, from its spinnerets, several strands of
silk which, when the breeze catches them, pluck the
spider into the air like a kite surfer. Migrating spiders
can travel long distances like this when the conditions
are right: they have been found on balloons at an
altitude of five kilometres, and have been reported to
have landed on ships in mid-ocean.

Ticknock, 17 November
Early this morning I climbed Ticknock with Teresa.
A high-pressure centre had been hanging over the
west coast for days, covering the country with low
cloud and bringing dull depressing weather and early
winter darkness. There was no horizon, and the
heavens and the Irish Sea were a seamless, uniform
pale grey. The mountain landscape was a dull brown,
but the wildlife we experienced more than made up
for it. As we climbed from the end of the forest road
towards Two Rock, we disturbed a flock of golden
plover grazing in the heather not far from the track,
perhaps the same flock that I had seen earlier in the
month. About a hundred birds took off spectacularly,
in a flowing formation, with an easily audible whoosh
of wings, leaving a chorus of plaintive calls hanging
on the still air. As we stood to watch, they wheeled
around like a single live thing and, showing their pale
undersides and then their brown backs, landed again
a bit farther away. In an attempt to get a closer look,
we crossed the heather slowly, but succeeded only

in unsettling them again. Off they went, this time higher and higher, and after wheeling a few times they seemed to set off for the other side of Glencullen valley, calling all the while. Soon the flock settled into a long arc, with what we thought of as the leaders at the centre, and a few stragglers back where the string of a bow might be. As we watched, an unusual thing happened; the stragglers made a 180° turn, and as soon as they were heading back towards us, the rest of the flock poured around effortlessly to follow them. They swept past us with a rush of wingbeats and flew farther down the valley. Shortly after, having reformed an arc, the same thing happened; the stragglers, which must have been the original leaders, turned back, with their undersides flashing, and drew the rest with them. This practice was continued all the time we watched, fascinated by the shapes they made in the sky as the formation, like a 'join the dots' puzzle, took on one shape after another, morphing smoothly from a dog's head to an aeroplane, to a prowling cat. They seemed to be obsessed by their aerobatic gyrations and in no hurry to land, and as they moved over to the other side of the valley and became a blurred, ghost-like form against the landscape backdrop, we walked on, hearing their calls for a long time afterwards.

Kilcop, 20 November

In spite of the fact that we have a kerosene boiler coming on for short periods twice a day when we are not there, it was cold in Kilcop, and it took a while to get the cottage comfortable. We had to stoke up our solid fuel stove, which we call Betsy, and in no time she was blasting away, eating logs. I warmed myself outside, trimming and cutting all the overhanging branches along the front hedge and laying the blackthorn bushes where they occur along that stretch. I spiked the back of my hand on a blackthorn, and although it was just one thorn, it was surprisingly painful. I finished the day sawing all the branches I had harvested into logs, and stacking them in the airing barn.

In recent years there has been an increase in appearances of whales and dolphins off the Waterford coast, so when we walk there we tend to keep a close eye on the sea. We were rewarded this evening during a stroll on the pier at Dunmore East when we saw three dolphins cavorting offshore. In the winter, shoals of herring often pass along the coast, and they can be followed by dolphins and whales. Humpbacks, fin whales and minke whales have been sighted at the mouth of Waterford Harbour, but these three dolphins were the first I have encountered on this coast. I would dearly love to see whales here. Apart from this incident, in our careful scanning of our coastal waters we have seen only seals, which can be difficult to spot. They are easily taken for buoys or lobster pot floats on the surface of the water, but closer examination – and binoculars are a must for walks along sea-coasts – might reveal a whiskered dog-like head, looking curiously around.

Other than in the very few remaining uninhabited corners of the country, there is no such thing as complete darkness any more in the Irish countryside. Although in Kilcop we are five miles from Waterford City, the glow of its lights reflected on the bottoms of clouds has increased greatly in recent years. The rhythmic flashes of Hook Lighthouse, a good thirteen kilometres away across the mouth of Waterford Harbour, can also be seen at night, skimming the cloud base.

The brilliance of the display of stars on a clear night, something long lost for city people, was still possible to enjoy up to a decade ago in the countryside, but today the illumination provided by farmyard floodlights or the borealis glow of nearby towns has made even the universe fade. We talk about 'light pollution' today, but it must have been a wonderful boon for country folk when rural electrification spread throughout Ireland in the 1930s, banishing the long, dark winter nights that cloaked the land in primordial darkness. The same electrification brought radio, television and labour-saving devices to the countryside, but it also brought an end to the old rural ethos that manifested itself in the stories told and songs sung around the cheering light of cottage fires. I imagine this old world reached back to a pre-Christian Ireland, and while momentous historical events occurred as the centuries passed and occasionally great armies marched nearby, the ordinary rural folk kept their heads down and got on with it. Their ancient, earth-based, climate-sensitive lifestyle continued uninterrupted, year in, year out, until quite recently. Electricity, the harbinger of technology and prosperity, tolled the final deathknell of this old mindset and, almost overnight, most rural people shook off the past and immersed themselves in the leading edge of the future. Dazzled by the light of progress and the power of technology, fairy bushes, the little people, crocks of gold, the old gods and

ancient heroes faded away, and old farming practices
went the same way.

In the early days in Kilcop, we had no television,
but the children got used to enjoying nights by the
fire. If neighbours called, it was fireside conversation
that filled our evenings, and our children took a
full part in this. One neighbour was always called
upon by the children to tell ghost stories about the
surrounding area, and he was happy to oblige, and
although his language could sometimes be salty, this
only added to the atmosphere. Many rural stories
seemed to hark back to the seventeenth century. One
that the children particularly liked to hear again
and again was about a nearby mansion, which in
Cromwell's time was a convent, and the story involved
six nuns being killed by the Cromwellian soldiers and
buried under the kitchen floor. A house still exists
there, and was always remarked upon by the children
when we passed by.

Glendoher, 26 November
This morning there was a little flock of redwings
grazing on our cotoneaster berries. When disturbed,
they all, as one, flew up into a nearby tree, and, just
like a Charles Tunnicliffe painting, they all perched
facing the same way, feathers fluffed up. The poet
in Thomas Hardy wrote about the disappearance of
berries in 'Birds at Winter Nightfall':

> Around the house the flakes fly faster,
> And all the berries now are gone
> From holly and cotoneaster
> Around the house. The flakes fly! – faster

Shutting indoors that crumb-outcaster
We used to see upon the lawn
Around the house. The flakes fly faster,
And all the berries now are gone!

Hellfire Hill, 27 November

The soundtrack at this time of year on the sheltered
side of the hill is a leafy one, the loud crunch of
leaves underfoot, the whispering, fragile rustle of
leaves falling through the branches, and the constant,
hissing rustle of the breeze through those still
clinging on. As a child I was told that you could make
a wish if you caught a falling leaf before it reached
the ground: I must have succeeded many times, but
cannot remember if what I wished came to pass. The
larches on the hillside have achieved a straw/gold
colour I don't recall noting before, the colour graded
and becoming paler towards the branch tips. Behind
the larches are dark, sombre green noble firs, tilting
their branches slightly upwards, as dignified and
graceful as the arms of a ballet dancer.

Even in this dry weather, the water from the
spring pond on the south side of the hill overflows
in a rivulet down the forestry road; the pond itself
was motionless today, without even a diving beetle
to catch the eye. The pond's rich and populous
ecological system has all but closed down, and it will
not awake until the spring.

Since the trees on the south side of the hill were
harvested a couple of years ago, the exposed forestry
to the north and east has suffered severe damage in
gales; great swathes of trees, acres in extent, have
been blown over, forming a dense, impenetrable

mess of trunks, branches and roots. The harvested area has already been vigorously recolonised with a thick growth of grasses, herbs and wildflowers that had lain fallow and hidden from the sun since the 1960s, when the trees were planted. Unfortunately, the ground has been replanted with the awful sitka spruce, and within a dozen years the herbage will be banished into the darkness again.

While the wind was keeping the small birds to the dark and sheltered recesses of the trees, there were large mixed flocks of a hundred or more crows, rooks and grey-backed crows quartering the hill; one such flock made an enthusiastic and spectacular dive bomb attack on the valley north of Piperstown Hill, birds jinking and weaving as they dropped from a height at considerable speed, some of them calling in voices that almost approximated to birdsong rather than the usual caws or croaks. At the tail end of the flock I spotted a lone wood pigeon, clearly with an identity crisis, gamely trying to keep up with his enthusiastic new friends.

The south side of the hill was well sheltered by a single row of wind-breaking trees, which give occasional views down to Piperstown Hill. Farther on, the beautiful, rich, rust-brown pine cones clustered on top of the noble firs had been got at by squirrels; some had just holes in them, while others had been eaten from the bottom to within an inch of the top, and resembled tree-top mushrooms. It is interesting that our native red squirrel, displaced so often by the imported grey, has taken such a liking to, and may be saved by, these imported conifers, which seem unsuitable for the grey.

Ticknock, 29 November

I escaped to the hills again this morning. I believe, or
should I say I have persuaded myself, that time spent
there considerably increases my writing productivity,
so I took an hour of 'time out' on Ticknock today.
Although there was not a breath of wind at low
altitude, I ascended the hill into a bitterly cold north-
westerly wind, increasing in strength as I went up.
At the windy cairn on the Fairy Castle it was strange
to see that down in Dublin Bay was another world:
the water beside the Pigeon House was mirror-like,
perfectly reflecting the tall chimneys.

There was no sign of deer in their usual place
on the eastern side of the hill, and other than the
twittering of unseen goldcrests in the conifers,
no birds braved the air. The entertainment today,
however, was the long visibility from the Fairy Castle –
in spite of mists and fogs up and down the Irish coast,
I could see, on the horizon to the right of Howth,
the ghostly image of South Barrule, a 48-metre-high
hill on the Isle of Man all of 140 kilometres away.
It is rare that the conditions allow a view of the Isle
of Man from here; I have seen it only once before.
Some years ago, from the top of Barrule, I could
see the undulations of the Wicklow Mountains on
the southern horizon, and Holyhead Mountain and
Snowdonia were also clearly in view. I find there is a
powerful magic in being able to oversee great swathes
of the nearby world.

Below, the ferry from Dublin Port was forging its
way out of the calm waters of the bay on its way to
Holyhead, and it was strange to think that I could see

both the ship and her destination; it would be at least another hour and a half before the people on the ship would catch sight of Wales.

December

Now let the weather do its worst,
With frost and blowing,
Rage like a bedlam wild and curst,
And have its fill of snowing.

– Amos Russel Wells, 'On December 21'

seagull

DECEMBER HAS FINALLY ARRIVED, heralded by a cold spell and lots of snow. We started lighting fires early in November and we are accustomed now to the comfort of the fireplace at evening time with our Kilcop logs giving off a bright, warming glow. Winter is still a bit of a novelty, and it will remain so until mid-January, when one begins to long again for shorter nights.

Glendoher, 2 December

We have had snow now for the fourth day in a row, and where it is undisturbed on the flat roof of the shed, it sits like a thick white mattress. Yesterday morning I noticed that the garden was criss-crossed with the footprints of a four-legged animal, I think a fox, which seems to have spent the night wandering around aimlessly. I imagine the snow cover must make finding food difficult, and the animal is probably desperate at this stage, though why it is hanging around our garden I do not know.

We have been putting out extra food on the feeder for the birds, but we don't normally put out food for foxes. This morning there were fresh prints that seemed to indicate that, perhaps early in the morning, the animal took a running series of two-metre-long strides down the garden to leap up onto the raised flowerbed, where the snow is chaotically disturbed and scattered with grey feathers. It looks as if the waiting paid off for the hungry fox, and he breakfasted today on wood pigeon.

Glendoher, 9 December

The snow has almost all melted, returning the prospect from the back window to its usual winter drabness. I was washing my teeth in the bathroom when I spotted, in the air over the field, a crow mobbing a buzzard. The big bird turned this way and that, and was surprisingly agile, swerving and diving out of the crow's reach. The buzzard circled twice around the field, and then, after almost coming straight at the bathroom window, soared up at the last minute to hover right over the garden. Toothbrush in hand, I had to get my face against the glass to keep him in sight. He circled the field once more, followed by his tormentor, before alighting on a conifer at the western end. Almost at once, crows, rooks, greybacks and magpies materialised from all directions, hurrying to converge on the unfortunate buzzard. There must have been twenty birds in all, some circling the tree and others perching, watching their quarry and cawing and rasping. Eventually, the buzzard got tired of it all, and, launching himself majestically into the air, flew slowly westwards across Ballyboden Road and disappeared. With that, the mob began to disperse, and quiet descended once more. It was interesting to see that the buzzard's tormentors seemed to give up the harassment as soon as the big bird left the field: do all these different members of the crow family have some territorial sense about that field?

All the plants in our little wild garden around the pond, which were specially selected to provide nectar and food for our insects and birds, have succumbed to winter's harshness, with the exception of the ivy. Elsewhere in the garden, I try to keep the ivy at bay – legions of exploratory tendrils come over the wall from the field and have to be dealt with before they establish themselves, under cover of other foliage, in the flowerbeds. Ivy is very effective at protecting itself, and seems to know how to hide under other bigger plants or to consort with and stay close and cosy to a plant that we actually want in the garden.

At the pond, however, I have encouraged one ivy plant to develop, frequently cutting it back when it strays beyond the area around the pond, and so now it has quite a thick woody trunk. With every plant around it deep in winter slumber, this ivy alone is performing a valuable seasonal service. Its flowers, which up until recently provided an abundant late nectar source for insects, have now been replaced by greenish berries, which will soon blacken and be full of goodness for the birds in the garden. They, in return, pay for this service by distributing ivy seeds.

Glendoher, 12 December

Today dawned with a gusty wind, and the colours of the early morning were spectacular. A pale blue sky was crossed by fast-moving bundles of cotton wool-like clouds which turned to peach when the early sun's rays reached them. Sunlight had not yet painted the tops of the Spinney, but seagulls flying westwards, high up, banking from side to side to counter the wind, were transfigured in a luminous pink.

Last week there was an invasion of seagulls in the back garden. We had left out some cereal on the flat roof of the shed, as we had done before, but this time it attracted as many as two dozen gulls. Not all of them descended to the roof; most of them, to the distress of the local birds, I imagine, circled the field, looking very menacing. I went out into the garden and drove them off with a great display of shouting and waving of arms that must have amused my neighbours. Today, looking out from my eyrie in the bathroom window, I noticed they were back again, circling the field purposefully, occasionally worried by a few grey-backed crows.

I am concerned about the increasing number of these large birds frequenting the sky over the field. But for the heron, they are by far the biggest birds we see from the kitchen window, bigger than the grey-backed crows and the frequently visiting ravens. When they start circling the field, they are clearly loitering with intent. I'm not sure what the intent is yet, but it can't be good for our smaller resident birds. While I often give out about magpies and their general disruptive and predatory activities, at least the magpies are local lads; the gulls are not from here – they are daily blow-ins – and I am sure they are up to no good. A householder a couple of streets away, for some reason, started feeding the gulls, and they used to line up on his and his neighbours' rooftops awaiting feeding time. The neighbours complained about the noise they made and the gull droppings on their clotheslines, and so the gulls' food kitchen closed down. During the period that they were being fed, however, it seems that they got used to the place, and are now targeting the area.

I don't know a lot about varieties of gulls, but I think the culprit bird in our case is the herring gull. It is intelligent and adaptable, and exists in very large numbers along the Dublin coast; they will travel up to thirty miles from their coastal roost to find food sources, which means we are well within their range. They are noisy and aggressive, and in recent times, probably because of the downturn in fishing activity at Howth, they seem to have decided to abandon their seaside clifftop and rock ledge homes and have begun to nest on urban rooftops. This has given rise to a number of problems, such as the build-up of their droppings, the blocking of gutters with their nesting materials, and damage to paint on cars. Even worse, I am told that the bacterial and fungal agents found in their droppings can carry a number of serious diseases, including meningitis, encephalitis and salmonella. Even if one wanted to, one cannot think of taking a shotgun to them, because they are protected under national and European wildlife acts.

Glendoher, 15 December
'Cold fog and frost: the numbed, frightened birds will not leave the trees, but chirrup feebly through the curtain to one another.' So wrote the poet Edward Thomas about birds in December. Although we cannot see it happening, as winter takes the landscape in its grip, many thousands of small birds die of cold or starvation. Some of the larger ones, such as the thrush, will migrate southwards as far as is necessary, to where there is no frost or snow. Our everyday garden residents that remain for the winter, such as the blue tits and the coal tits, will suffer large losses, some of them becoming too weak to even make it to the bird table. This is why birds such as the blue tit produce so many offspring, often ten to a clutch. Blackbirds and robins have multiple broods, and by the time autumn comes, their offspring, in spite of predation of other birds and cats, are everywhere. By December, however, the shortage of food and the competition for rapidly decreasing resources means that only the strongest survive. The rest are what scientists call 'the doomed surplus', and they simply disappear. But for the odd frozen corpse, one rarely sees the dead body of a small bird, because they are swiftly dealt with by hungry insects and worms.

We like to think that putting out food for the birds in wintertime will help, and that a bird table will probably rescue a few of the weaker birds. Some scientists say, however, that keeping the weaker birds alive through the winter may reduce the strength of the gene pool, and ultimately may lead to local extinction. I find this concerning. It is true that nature has its way of running things, and there is the possibility that if we get involved too much, we could disrupt the natural way of things. I have to admit that our main reason for putting out food for the birds is to have the pleasure of watching them, and seeing what unusual birds our table will attract.

Glendoher, 19 December
There have been more flurries of snow showers, and the declivities of the hills are still etched out in frost. We love the texture and crunch of walking in snow, and how it dresses the outdoor world in a white blanket, muffling all sounds. I find it hard to understand why a snow-covered landscape is always a sight of beauty for us; there must be, deep in our Irish peasant DNA, a detestation of snowy weather. A mere couple of centuries ago snowy winters meant death for many in the community, particularly amongst the old; it is difficult to imagine poor peasants rushing out of their mud cabins on a snowy morning to make a snowman and have a snowball fight with their neighbour. For us, snow brings warm memories of childhood, and of Christmas, although a white Christmas is a very rare event in Ireland. Perhaps a white Christmas is partly a construct of English Christmas cards, which were rarely without snow, robins and mistletoe. We didn't have any Irish-designed cards until the early twentieth century when the works of Jack B. Yeats and George Fagan were

used as illustrations. Mistletoe certainly didn't feature in these, although the parasitic plant is named by the author and naturalist Pliny the Elder as being sacred to the Celts.

Ticknock, 20 December
It was too icy to drive into the hills this morning, so I left my car in Marlay Park and headed south, following the Wicklow Way up onto Kilmashoge Mountain. It was glorious as the sun rose over the forest-fringed rim of the hill ahead. Under a pale blue sky packed with puffy, snow-filled clouds, the city looked beautiful below, its snowy surfaces gleaming. Carlingford Mountain, rising above the northern horizon and backed by a chorus of ghostly white Mourne summits, seemed only a short distance away. On the long straight climb to where the Wicklow Way turns south, the low sun stretched my shadow back down the forestry road for a full fifty metres. A raven flew over, high up, and yet again I asked myself where are individual birds going when they pass by? If one watches the sky for more than a couple of minutes one will not fail to see birds passing, some quite high, alone or in pairs, all flying, purposefully, in a specific direction. These journeys do not seem to be short trips from roost to feeding places, and I wonder where they are going with such purpose, and where have they come from? I will have to look into the matter to see if anyone has done a study on the longer distance movements of ordinary birds.

For a short while it had looked as if it would snow again, but the rising sun seemed to clear away the dark clouds, and so I continued, climbing to the

saddle between Tibradden and the Fairy Castle along
the Dublin Mountains Way path. The trees were
thickly frosted where the sun had not got at them: it
is interesting to note that the heat of the sun, even
in these sub-zero temperatures, is considerable,
and quickly melts the intricate frost flowers that
coat the foliage. A frigid wind must have come from
the south-east during the night, growing brilliantly
gleaming razor blades of ice on the branches of the
trees, and I came across one amazing clump of gorse
that was a confection of snowy delight.

Although the north-facing heathery landscape was
picturesquely white and there were frozen great drifts
against hedges and banks, the frosted snow was thin
on the ground. The pathway was scattered with the
spoor of early-rising mountain inhabitants going this
way and that, but other than birds flying by, high up,
there was no sign of life. There were also the boot-
prints of an early walker, who was accompanied by a
dog that frequently darted in and out of the heather
to the sides of the path. I had to keep a careful eye to
the ground, because I was encountering, in places,
treacherous sheets of black ice concealed under the
thin covering of snow. It would be so easy, without
crampons, to slip and come down on the rock-hard
ground, so, when in doubt, I diverted into the safety
of white-frosted heather to bypass dangerous-looking
patches.

The ascent to the Fairy Castle was in brilliant
sunshine and I was lucky I had my sunglasses in my
rucksack. I was delighted to reach the summit: in the
darker early morning I had thought I might make
it to Kilmashoge, but here I was, much farther and
much higher, in a relatively short time. The cairn was

encrusted in ice, and all the stones on the north side were beautifully dressed with crystal wings.

In spite of the sunshine, it was bitterly cold at the top, and after briefly revelling in the beauty of the sea and sky, I began my descent. Maybe I was too relaxed at this stage, because I slipped on unseen ice and went down with a thump twice on the way down, but luckily nothing was hurt but my pride. As I went, I caught up with the man and his dog, the owners of the footprints I had spotted earlier. He was a Kerryman from Cloghane on the Dingle Peninsula, and turned out to be a cousin of the late Nora Murphy, who had the pub at Brandon Pier, and whom I had known. When I asked him how, being from such a wonderful place, he found living in Dublin, he told me that he didn't mind as long as he can get up into the hills. We parted at the Kilmashoge turn, and I continued down to the public road. After an eleven-kilometre winter walk I arrived back in Marlay Park, slightly footsore, but feeling on top of the world.

Glendoher, 21 December
I found Freddy, the remaining shubunkin goldfish, in the pond this morning, frozen solid in the skin of ice that covers it. I can't understand this, because when water cools, it contracts in volume, and the warmer water, being heavier, sinks to the bottom. This is usually where fish resort to in freezing temperatures, so I cannot imagine why Fred got himself frozen at the surface.

A flock of redwings flew over the house today, putting me in mind of years ago when we used to be visited by congregations of redwings and fieldfares;

unfortunately, after an apartment block was built next door, the fieldfares didn't come back. The name redwing is a misnomer: this bird of the thrush family has an orange/red streak on its flanks, but not on its wings. Sometimes the red streak is not clearly visible anyway, and it is better, for identification, to rely on the broad white streak that the bird has over its eyes. In December 2010 we had heavy snowfalls that left over 300mm in the garden and gave every bush a thick white hat. We continued to feed our local birds, although what was put out was soon covered with snow. There were still plenty of berries left when a flock of redwings descended on the front garden and spent two days foraging there. The snow was concealing so many berries from them that I had to go out and beat it off the bushes to allow the beautiful little thrushes get at them. When they left, the bushes had been stripped of every berry.

This year, after the rains of the late spring and the long hot days of an exceptional summer, there was a particularly plentiful show of berries on every bush and tree in the garden. Our domestic birds – thrushes, blackbirds and wood pigeons – appreciated the largesse of the year, and have been feeding, in particular, on our pyracantha bushes, which a pair of thrushes used for nesting earlier in the year.

There have been siskins in the garden for the last week. There is a flock of five, possibly a family, and they hang around in the bare branches of the birch, often in the company of a pair of friendly greenfinches. It's very early for the siskins, but Michael Viney's column in *The Irish Times* has mentioned reports of quite a number of passerines turning up unusually early this year. We have had continuous gales for the last month or so and this may be having an effect on migrations.

We took a trip out to Bull Island in north Dublin to see the wintering birds. Even before we got there, we could see many great flocks of geese, ducks and waders from the coast road; there have to be very few capital cities that have a bird sanctuary so close to the centre. Bull Island, about five kilometres long, is a fortuitous result of a great wall being built in the eighteenth century to protect, from the build-up of sandbanks, the entry to Dublin port. In the 1930s its beach, dunelands and mudflats became Ireland's first bird sanctuary, and it achieved the status of a UNESCO Biosphere Reserve in 1981, making it a world-class destination for birdwatchers. I find it the easiest place to experience, close up, the variety and great numbers of bird species wintering in the Dublin area. The mudflats, which at first sight look lifeless, are in fact teeming with life just below the surface. Unlike sand, which is washed ashore by the sea, most mudflats are made up of river silt, transported downstream and dumped as the water slows to a halt when it meets the incoming sea. This mud is full of bacteria that are fed upon by a great abundance of worms and invertebrates, and these creatures provide rich food for the birds. One cubic metre of estuary mud can contain, in addition to tiny shrimp and large and complex ragworms, as many as 60,000 spire-shell mud snails, all of them favourites of birds.

No matter how often I do it, I find the experience of a winter visit to Bull Island hugely uplifting; the numbers and species of birds one sees is simply astounding. We parked on the causeway and took a long walk out along the island, marvelling at how fortunate the people of Dublin are to have such a place on their doorstep. You don't have to be in Dublin, however, to experience the spectacle of thousands of birds arriving every year to winter in Ireland. The sea or our inland lakes and rivers are natural habitats that are rich in wildlife, particularly in winter, when they attract an abundance of geese and wildfowl from the northern countries which spend the winter in the relative warmth of Ireland.

Glendoher, 23 December
A buzzard, possibly the same one that has been here a few times recently, came gliding around the field this morning, and was, as usual, mobbed by magpies and greybacks. He eventually settled on a low branch of a beech tree in the Spinney, where the magpies continued to annoy him, although he seemed to ignore them. The field has lain fallow for nearly forty years, and must have a large population of field mice, some of which winter in our shed, and it is perhaps these that attract the big bird.

Glendoher, 27 December
St Stephen's Day was mild and sunny. It reminded me of what a wonderful climatically gentle country we live in, and of another St Stephen's Day a couple of decades ago when I climbed with some companions, through thick cloud, to the top of one of the Dublin mountains. Imagine our delight when we emerged from the top of the clouds onto a summit basking in brilliant sunshine. It was hot, and we sat down there in our shirtsleeves as if on an island surrounded by a

white sea, looking out at the islands of other nearby summits. The Irish winter can be strange.

As the busyness of Christmas passes and the darkness of winter deepens, my mind turns to less than uplifting thoughts about the future of the earth on which we live. I never remember seeing so many articles and television programmes about aspects of the extinction of species, the degradation of our environment and global warming as I have during this past year. Everywhere one turns, there are photos of honey bees, butterflies and burning rainforests. Unfortunately, the tiny percentage of the population who take an interest in these matters and want to live as sustainably as possible by doing the simple things, such as turning off unneeded lights, not wasting food or water, and recycling as much as possible, cannot affect the operation of the Gulf Stream. And what about the millions, perhaps billions, of fellow humans who do not have the leisure time available to them to think about these things because they are scrabbling and scraping to simply survive, one day at a time. In a caring world, all these people would be catered for, but that would involve us rich westerners agreeing to lower our living standards and share our wealth, and I don't see that happening any time soon. Nor do I see the human race's lemming-like rush to obliteration slowing down. Perhaps only global catastrophe will bring a halt. When these kinds of thoughts invade my sense of well-being, I go out into the garden and watch the birds!

In spite of the darkness it brings, it is at least a comforting thought that December brings not only the end of a year, but the beginning of a new year, although no remarkable change is discernible after the 21st. Over the last few days, however, the dull and dismal weather has been brightened up considerably by the numbers and variety of avian visitors to the back garden. This morning, for instance, goldfinches have been vying with redpolls, siskins and greenfinches for a perch on the nut dispensers, making a colourful and busy display. We are becoming so used to the five cock goldfinches that have been everyday visitors for the last week that we no longer exclaim about them.

Today I was delighted to see a curlew flying over, quite high, its long and curved beak unmistakable: it's a bird that used to be plentiful but is currently reported as being yet another endangered species. It seems clear, however, that many people are becoming aware of the widespread dangers to our natural world, and are beginning to adopt more sustainable lifestyles. I am hopeful that next year will see our government and businesses follow suit. Can spring be far behind?

beech mast and leaves

INDEX